REMEMBER
Eternity
I Am That I Am

J. E. STARKS-BROWN

authorHOUSE®

AuthorHouse™
1663 Liberty Drive
Bloomington, IN 47403
www.authorhouse.com
Phone: 1 (800) 839-8640

Published by AuthorHouse 10/02/2018

ISBN: 978-1-5462-6281-7 (sc)
ISBN: 978-1-5462-6280-0 (e)

Library of Congress Control Number: 2018911868

Print information available on the last page.

FOREWORD

In these perilous and uncertain times, there remains one undeniable fact that we all must face and that is Eternity. As we live our everyday lives, year in and year out, we are ever moving closer to the era where time will be an extinct entity. In our human natures, we tend to view Eternity as a fact that is eons away or something to be dealt with after we tend to our own temporal agendas.

The Word of God leaves no doubt about the two eternal destinations that we have the options to choose from. Eternal reward in Heaven or eternal damnation in Hell leaves no choice to the reasonable mind and this being said, it only makes sense to "Remember Eternity".

In this society, we are bombarded with countless winds of doctrine that have forms of godliness while denying the power thereof which is a danger to the eternal soul. Ephesians 4:5 (KJV) plainly states that there is One Lord, one faith, one baptism. This one Lord, Jesus Christ, commanded us in St. Matthew 28:19 to be baptized in the name of the Father (Jesus), the name of the Son (Jesus) and the name of the Holy Ghost (Jesus), not His titles. This was confirmed through the Apostle Peter on the Day of Pentecost (Acts 2:38), when three thousand souls were added on the Birth Day of the Church. The ingredients of genuine godly sorrow or repentance from sin, water baptism in the name of Jesus for the remission or removal of sin, coupled with the baptism of the Holy Ghost. The undeniable evidence of this second birth experience is the speaking in other tongues as the Spirit of God gives the utterance. There is no substitute for this awesome encounter with God that empowers the born again believer to overcome the sinful Adamic nature that we are all enter into this world with. It is not to be scoffed at or minimized by those who would downplay its significance or importance.

"Remember Eternity" opens with eighteen year old Janice Scott who impulsively leaves her home in Washington D.C. to join her cousins in Des Moines Iowa. While harboring a secret, she develops new relationships and begins to encounter situations that ultimately transform her from an angry and cynical teen-ager into a new creature in God. As one life touches another, circumstances evolve into a myriad of events that in time give God the glory for His wonderful works to the children of men.

Janice discovers the power of Agape' love through those that are Spirit filled while enduring several life changing hardships that forever change her perspective on life. Through these adversities, she begins to experience a father-daughter relationship that she was deprived of during her unstable childhood and this in turn enriches her spirit in a way that had been before unimaginable. Because of the God given wisdom and compassion of her surrogate father Douglas, she learns how to depend on the God of her salvation as she simultaneously begins to give of herself to others.

"Remember Eternity" is an intimate look into a family's struggles, victories, trials and tribulations of the righteous which are all a part of the sanctified set apart life that God is calling for in these troubling and stressful times.

INTRODUCTION

"Remember Eternity", as its title suggests, is a reminder to us all that there is life beyond this one in which we now live. It is a fictional look into the lives of not so ordinary Spirit filled people in the process of making preparations for Eternity. Set in the city of present day Des Moines, Iowa, the intention of "Remember Eternity" is to help the reader get beyond what we see with our natural or carnal minds and to become focused on the spiritual and that which is eternal.

The story line revolves around the day to day challenges in the African -American family of Frances Michaels, her son Paul and three daughters, Irene, Christine and Donna; their spouses, Jane, Douglas, James and Randy. As the mother of four and grandmother of forty-one, Frances is recognized as a matriarchal symbol of God given wisdom, and full of life changing experiences. She is ever nurturing, advising and whether solicited or no, her words are lovingly accepted with gratitude. As her young twenty something neices Sheila, Ruth, and high school senior 'Nita come into play, relationships flourish in the midst of adverse circumstances.

Paul, the stern and serious high school principal, Douglas the prosperous insurance executive with a miraculous transformation saved from the streets testimony, James the successful arcitech and Randy the pubic transit operator all come together to create a wealth of events and situations. As Paul, Christine and their spouses face the challenges of their interracial marriages, they ultimately become stronger in their faith in God. He becomes their battle axe and strength in adversity when outside sources challenge their relationships. Sensitive issues arise but are successfully overcome by proven spiritual weapons of warfare which is the basic foundation and theme of "Remember Eternity."

It is intended to reinforce spiritual perspectives in an increasingly anti-Christ society and although unpopular and often tedious, the life of Bible based holiness will eternally prevail.

In "I Am That I Am", this family is faced with situations that only the One Almighty God will prevail through His anointed vessels. Incurable disease as well as so called impossible situations arise as the Great "I Am" continues to prove Himself sovereign and fulfills the scripture in His word that declares "For with God, nothing shall be impossible."

CHAPTER 1

SUNDAY, JUNE 7

"Michael has his phone number and he's plannin' on stayin' in contact with him because if he doesn't, there's no tellin' what might happen." Douglas remarked, referring to Andre' Sunday night with Terry, Janice, Sheila and Frances in the family room at Chris and James' house.

"And that's what happens if you don't feed a new baby, if you leave it to itself, it'll die and you can't let that happen." Frances said as Chris came in. "Feelin' any better?" She asked her.

"A little, I figured out that I've been tryin' to do too much and it's catchin' up with me." She said as she sat down. "Are James and Irene almost done over there?"

"She called a minute ago, they've got the truck loaded up and ready to go in the mornin' so by this time tomorrow, it'll be a done deal." Douglas said as he checked his phone.

"I might be able to go over there and help 'em get unpacked, I'll see how it goes tomorrow."

"If you don't feel like it, 'Nita can go in your place." Frances told her. "That's why she's here, a little work won't hurt her."

"So how did it go, don't leave anything out." Chris told Terry.

"It turned out better than I thought it would." She said, in awe at what had happened.

"One of the guys that helped put her in the hospital was there." Sheila said, speaking for her.

"You are kiddin.'" She said as she turned the t.v. volumn down with the remote. "You're gonna have to back up and start from the beginnin.'"

"I told Anthony where we were gonna be tonight and he let him know about it." Terry said. "We work together at the store and I still don't know how they hooked up but it is what it is."

"Anthony came to the hospital the night it happened and he called me and asked if it was alright for Andre' to come." Douglas said. "I gave him a business card that night and held on to it and that's the only reason I knew he was gonna be there."

"Chris it was almost surreal." Sheila told her. "This whole thing is sort of mind bogglin' to me." She said pausing as she tried to organize her thoughts.

"We don't have anything but time Sheila, it's all good." Chris said, fascinated.

"Tell her what happened Douglas, you were up there." Sheila told him after Terry got up and went outside.

"Is she alright?"

"I do the same thing, when me and the Lord are havin' a moment, I have to be by myself." Janice remarked.

"Okay Douglas, cut to the chase, what happened?" Chris insisted.

"We were sittin' in the back together and he asked me if he could go up there to talk to her." He began. "And that was okay with me as long as I was up there with him, it wasn't gonna be any other way."

"I love it, keep goin.'" Chris said, laughing with him.

"She was wrappin' it up so I felt like it was okay." "I walked up there and he asked her if she remembered him and she didn't say anything for a second like she was thinkin' about it." He continued. "She backed up to make sure that I had her back, then I think it started to come back to her."

"And you could almost hear the grass growin' in there, it was unreal." Sheila said.

"Tell me about it." "he was up there cryin' like a baby and he could tell that she was startin' to remember him and that's when he just came out and asked her to forgive him or what went on that night."

"Are you serious?"

"It gets better, believe me." Douglas said as he recalled the moment. "He took her off guard because I think that was the last thing she expected to hear."

"What did you tell her, we couldn't hear that part of it." Sheila asked him. "And if you don't wanna say, I understand that but this is just too good and I want all of the details."

"I told her to talk to him so that the Lord would use her and that's when she said that she had to forgive him because God forgave her and that's when he really lost it."

"Now I'm mad because I wasn't there." Chris said as 'Nita came in with Annette.

"She won't go to anybody but you daddy, here you go." She said as she put her on his lap. "And who lost it, I'm bein' nosy."

"One of the guys that was at the party with Terry came to hear her talk tonight and when he asked her to forgive him for what went on, it really affected him when she set him free if that's the way you wanna put it." Sheila told her as she sat down between she and Janice.

"That's exactly what happened and most people aren't used to that." Douglas said. "That's probably why he reacted like he did, he literally hit the floor like he couldn't believe what she said to him." He told Chris.

"So that was when you and Michael took him out wasn't it?" Sheila asked him.

"It was because whenever you see a soul under the power of God like that, you can't just walk away and hope they'll be okay." He began. "I could tell by the way he didn't care how he looked and acted in front of all those people that he was for real." "He was serious; when we got him behind closed doors and after he found out that we weren't out to get him because of who she is, he let it all hang out."

"Did he really?" Sheila asked with compassion in her voice.

"He did, he was tellin' us things that went on that we really didn't need to know but if it was helpin' him, it was just one of those things that we had to deal with."

3

"Michael told us that he reminded him of the way he was and after he told him to give it up, that's when he got his breakthrough." Sheila said as Terry came back in.

"You have got to be kiddin'." Chris said, shaking her head.

"This guy was the picture of what repentance looks like if there's a such thing." Douglas said. "And I'm findin' out more and more that it's the people that haven't heard about this that are the ones that seem to come through the quickest."

"I've heard that too." Sheila said. "What do you think is the reason for that?"

"You can't generalize about that but I think people that hear the truth all of their lives and don't know anything else tend to be numb and desensitized by it." "Then after so long, it just goes in one ear and out the other and it doesn't have the same effect that it does for somebody that's hearin' it for the first time."

"Like Irene huh?"

"Exactly." "And I asked her one day not too long after I got my help why she didn't have the Holy Ghost yet." "I didn't understand why she didn't didn't have this after knowin' about it all of her life."

"Because she had a stubborn streak a mile long and it wasn't until Paul talked to her that she seemed to get the message." Frances said. "And I've been sittin' here listenin' to what went on and not sayin' much because I'm so happy about how the Lord is showin' up for you young people." She continued. "If you keep lettin' the Lord lead you, you're gonna see more of the same things happen." She said with faith and authority as she put her around Terry who had sat down next to her. "And that's one of the best best reasons for somebody to stay in touch with this young man because when he gets a god foot hold and really learns about what he has now, there's no tellin' how many souls he'll be able to help."

"It's kind of a chain reaction thing and I'm sittin' here still tryin' to figure out this 2nd Chance thing." Sheila commented then.

"I was just about to ask you what happened with that." Terry told her.

"When we left here this afternoon, Michael went with me to try to find out exactly where this place is." She began. "We put the address in his G.P.S. and this place is two blocks from the church where we were tonight." "Two short little blocks and we could tell that this buildin' used to be a school and I found out yesterday when I called that it's a half way house for women that are startin' over from things, you know what I mean?"

She nodded.

"So we sat out in the parkin' lot for a while because I don't think just anybody can get in the doors without a code." She continued. "Then after about ten minutes, one of those fifteen passenger vans pulled up and lets all of these people off and that's when I decided to walk over there and tell 'em about what was goin' on at seven." She said, laughing at herself. "Then I told 'em if they wanted to come, they were more than welcomed to."

"You always did have a bold streak in you that used to make me wanna work you over." Chris told her. "She used to live with us and the crazy stuff that went on was unreal." She told Terry.

"I know that I was crazy but I figured why not, that was my chance that opened up to meet some new people so I went for it." She said. "And Douglas I remembered what you were prayin' in here before we left."

"Tell me about it ma'am."

"What I remember hearin' was the way you were askin' the Lord to use us for the sake of souls and those women needed to hear about what God will do for you when you believe Him." Sheila said after a moment.

"And you know it, it was a combination of believin' what you hear and a spirit of repentance that caused the Lord to move on Andre' and give him the Holy Ghost." Douglas said. "He probably didn't understand most of what she was talkin' about but it's not always about what you comprehend, it's your faith that moves God."

"I know that I didn't understand all of what Michael was tellin' me about what happened to him, but I didn't really have a choice but to believe it because of how different he was." Terry said.

"And that pretty much proves my point, when those two things come together, you're gonna see results every time."

"So did anybody get a chance to talk to him before he left?" Chris asked him.

"We did but you know how it feels right after you receive the Holy Ghost, you're in another world." "We explained to him what actually happened and he seemed to understand but he has both of our numbers and we have his so we're definitely gonna stay in contact with him."

"Good deal because I would hate to see him fall through the cracks because nobody would take the time to stay with him." Sheila said. "But I've got somethin' else that I can't shake off and I need to hear somebody's else's input."

"Go for it, we're listenin'."

"I'm really startin' to think that that woman that we met at Gringo's was an angel and I'm serious as a heart attack." Sheila said as she thought back to the experience with Ruth and Terry."

"Quit lyin' Sheila." 'Nita told her.

"I'm not, you know that I don't lie."

"I know you don't but how come you think that?"

"Because I've talked to two different people that are connected to this place, and both of 'em have told me that they don't have anybody named Kim on their staff." Sheila said as she got the business card from her wallet and showed it to her.

"When I walked into the restroom she was sittin' there like she was waitin' on me or somethin.'" Terry said. "She was really kind of different, you know what I mean?"

"She was because who in the world is gonna ask if they can come sit in a booth with total strangers like she did?" "Who does that?"

"Did they tell you about the scripture that says not to forget to entertain strangers because some people have been with angels and didn't know it?" Frances asked Terry.

"That's in the bible?" She asked, shocked.

"I'm gonna let you read it for yourself and Sheila I can't say that for sure honey but nothin' is impossible with God." Frances told her as she picked her bible up from the end table then.

"And every time I ask Patty about that day with Marie, she keeps sayin' that it was an angel that told her to go downstairs and that's when she found her in the bathroom." Janice said then. "She said that she saw it."

"That is so crazy, I had no idea that stuff like this really happens." Terry said in astonishment.

"Read this for me and tell me what you think." Frances said as she showed her the first two verses of Hebrews thirteenth chapter.

"Let brotherly love continue." "Be not forgetful to entertain strangers: for thereby some have entertained angels unawares." Terry read slowly to make sure she would get an understanding of the scripture in front of her.

"I keep thinkin' about that scripture and I can't think of any other explanation for this Kim lady." Sheila said." "I even asked a couple of those women that came tonight if they knew her and nobody has ever heard of her."

"Tell me this Sheila Scott." Douglas said a moment later.

"Here comes somethin' deep." She said.

"Not necessarily, just hear me out." He said.

"Okay sir." She said, starting to laugh. "Are you about to shoot my theory down?"

"Not at all, that's not what I do because who am I to say one way or another?" He asked her. "But what I'm a little curious about is what happened in the first place to make you think that way?"

"Number one, like I said, who in their right mind would ask to sit in a booth with people that they don't even know Douglas?"

"I wouldn't but it takes all kinds, people are doin' some bold and crazy stuff out there." "But I will give you that one, that's pretty much unheard of."

"Number two, she didn't order anything to eat once she sat down with us." "She sat down and listened to what we were talkin' about and it was mainly about what Terry had been through." "She saw her in the restroom and wanted to know what she was cryin' about and that was when she asked if she could come and sit with us in our booth because she wanted to hear all about it." "Terry was havin' a moment as Janice just said."

"And so on and so on." Douglas said.

"Excuse me if I'm not makin' much sense but I just can't get away from it and maybe I'm wrong; it might be just a concidence but I don't think so."

"Then when she got up all of a sudden and left that fifty dollar bill on the table for our checks, it was like, what's goin' on with this lady?" Terry said.

"You didn't mention that part of it." Douglas said then.

"See what I mean?" Sheila asked him. "And that's when she handed her this card." She said as she handed it to him.

"And everybody that you've talked to that works at this place doesn't know anything about her?"

"Nothin' Douglas, it's really strange."

"It's not if she was what you say she was and it's things like that that let us know how real all of this is." He told her. "And if she was the Lord's way of gettin' those souls over there to hear and see what went on, then it's all a good thing."

"Case closed huh?"

"If that's your gut feelin' and I wouldn't let anybody talk me out of it because it's a possibility." He said as Irene and James came in then.

"So are they ready to come out to no man's land?" Frances asked them.

"They can't wait, they're gettin' up at four in the mornin' to get this done so anybody that's available, get ready for a long day." Irene said as she took Annette from Douglas.

"That's my cue, I need to go to bed right now so I can be ready to do what I have to do because this is about to be a three ring circus out here, you heard it here first." 'Nita said as she got up. "And we're gonna need all of the angels we can get, watch and see."…

JUNE 9, TUESDAY

"Man I remembered that you work nights so I didn't wanna call you too early." Andre' remarked Tuesday morning after Michael let him in the front door.

"My off nights are Monday and Tuesday so don't worry about it, I went to bed last night." Michael said as they started towards the kitchen. "Have you had breakfast?" He asked him as he slowly sat down at the table a minute later.

He shook his head as he purposely kept his head down as if ashamed to be in Michael's presence. "I mean the last couple of days, I haven't even felt like eatin' anything, I'm still tryin' to figure it all out man." He admitted.

"Sometimes you can't but the main thing is all of the stuff in your past is your past." "It was all wiped out on Sunday because you believed God." Michael told him as he down aross from him. "And I know about that feelin', it's almost lke you can't understand how you went this long without knowin' about the Holy Ghost."

"That's what I'm talkin' about and I almost didn't bother about comin' with Anthony but he talked me into it." He began as he kept his eyes downward, avoiding eye contact with Michael. "For a couple of weeks, he kept tellin' me how I had to see your sister to believe it so I just went with him because he kept talkin' about it."

"Are you serious?"

"He said man, somethin' happened to her." "He told me about the guy that would show up at the store every Friday night right before the store closed and they's always leave together after he'd hand her a fifty dollar bill."

"She told me about him." Michael said.

"Then the same week that she came back to work after she got out of the hospital, he showed up like he always did and she told him straight up that she wasn't available." "Anthony couldn't believe it, he kept sayin', I don't know this girl any more."

"And that's what the spirit of God does, it changes you and I don't know a whole lot yet because it hasn't been that long since this happened to me." Michael said as he turned on the coffee maker that was sitting on the table. "I moved up here back in April from St. Louis after I lost my job down there and when I look back on that now, it was one of the best things that could've happened to me." "I called Douglas and told him what was goin' on and the rest is history as they say."

"Man that dude knew just what to and say and do to help me get over and when I get a chance to talk to him again, I have to tell him."

"He knows how to talk to people because of where he used to be, he was a street rat that did any and everything out there." Michael said. "And he hasn't forgotten how the Lord got him out of all of that so he uses his expereience to help that anybody that needs it."

"You would never know it by the way he was talkin' to me." Andre' commented, shaking his head a little. "I mean he was sayin' stuff that was kickin' me in my gut and I had never seen him before Sunday." He said in amazement.

"He doesn't know that much about you but God knows everything and He knows how to hook you up with people that can say and do that'll blow your mind man."

"I got my mind blown on Sunday, I know that much." He said as he recalled his experience. "And if I hadn't come to that church to hear her, this wouldn't have happened to me."

"So was it somethin' that said that stood out more than anything else that really helped you?"

"When she started talkin' about how she asked God to forgive her for the way she had been livin' for most of her life was what made me know she wasn't playin' around." He said as his voice trembled. "And if all of that happened for her, why couldn't happen for me too?" "And I'm still tryin' to put it all together."

"Then when you start to see how different you act and feel, you'll really start to get it." Michael told him. "And livin' this way is not always easy but that lifestyle out there wasn't easy either but the difference is the power that you have now that you didn't have before."

"So is that how your sister was able to walk away from that quick money without a problem?"

"She might've thought about it for a second or two but she didn't have to do what she was used to doin' because the power of the of the Holy Ghost that kept her out of trouble." Michael said. "She told me that she was even shocked at herself and I think it was the Lord showin' her just what she has now."

"It has to be God because I could tell by the way she was operatin' she knew what she was doin.'" "She knew how to get you and I'm just keepin' it real man."

"We have to keep it real because it's just life." Michael remarked. "But like we were sayin' on Sunday, we know what she was about so some of what happened was a lot of her own doin' but we're movin' on from all of that." He added as he attempted to elevate the subject of their conversation. "This is your new start and the closer you are to the Lord, the better off you'll be."

"How do you do that, God is off somewhere in the universe." "Andre' said after thinking about Michael's last statement."

"But He just gave you His spirit and it's in you so don't think of Him as somethin' way out there because He's everywhere."

"So that's what I've been feelin'?"

"He's there, believe me, we heard you and you heard it yourself didn't you?"

"I thought I was losin' it or somethin' but I remembered what she said happened to her and then it clicked."

"And I'll tell you the same thing that Douglas told me." Michael said. "He told me that there's nothin' more important than your relationship with the Lord because when that's in the right place, everything else will fall into place." "And that whole thing in a nutshell means to pray a lot and read what He has to say in this here." He said as he slightly lifted his bible up from the table where it was sitting near the coffee maker. "This will get you through anything and everything that might hit you."

"Man I had no idea that was even possible, I feel like I'm back in kindergarten."

"But that's okay, we all started out somewhere and it pays to listen to people that have been through some stuff." Michael said as he thought about Frances. "If it hadn't been for people that cared about what happened to me, I wouldn't be here and that's why we gave you our phone numbers so you can stay in contact with us."

"Man I thank you for that and all I know right now is that I feel a hundred per cent better about things because all of that other stuff is out of my life."

"There's nothin' else like it and when you try to explain it to other people, you can't think of the right words to describe it, you can't compare it to anything else."

"You got that right, I've been high and drunk and all of that but none of that stuff was like what happened to me Sunday night."

"And that's the awesome thing about it, you don't need that stuff any more because the Holy Ghost takes the appetite for all of that away, believe it or not."

"I'm startin' to really believe it because I can tell already somethin' is different." He said as Michael's phone rung then.

"Mornin' Miss Barbara, what's up?" He asked after her name appeared on the screen.

"Are you up and awake young man?"

"Yes ma'am I am, what can I do for you?"

"What are your plans for the next couple of hours?"

"I don't really have anything planned, do you have somethin' for me to do?"

"You're pretty strong aren't you?"

"I can get the job done when I have to but you don't have to be afraid to ask me for help, that's why I gave you my number." He told her. "And I even have somebody else here to help me if it's really major thing Miss Barbara. He said as Andre' gave him a thumbs up.

"Then that's even better because I have a few heavy boxes down in my basement that are full of Phillip's things that I'm ready to let go of." She said. "I've been thinkin' about what your brother told me the last time he was here and it's just time to move on and think about myself."

"So do you remember what's down there?"

"I really don't because it's been so long but it's time for me to do what I have to do." "If it's clothes, I might be able to donate to a shelter or somewhere like that but we'll just have to wait and see." She said with sadness in her voice.

"Do you need for us to come now?"

"If you can, I'll be waitin' on you."

"This might be a little deep but sometimes it's like that." Michael remarked after he ended the call. "This lady lives one street over from here; her son and Douglas were good friends and he died in a motorcycle accident a little over twenty years ago." Michael explained.

"And she still has his stuff in her house?"

"She's been holdin' on to anything he had for all of this time because she doesn't have anybody else in her life basically." Michael said. "But here's the thing, I'm learnin' how God works things out."

"Okay." Andre' said as he became distracted by his thoughts then.

"Did I say somethin', you look like somebody just kicked you in the gut."

"Did you say her son was killed on a motorcycle?"

"A little over twenty years ago, Douglas saw it happen because they were together." "Why, what are you thinkin'?"

"Did he ever tell you what his name was?" He cautiously asked him.

"His name was Phillip Mason, I've heard him talk about it more than once because it was after that accident that he got himself together." "That whole thing was like his turnin' point, you know what I mean?"

"Man I think that was my father." Andre' said after a moment as he tried to process the thought.

"Hold up, back up a minute." Michael told him. "How old are you, nineteen, twenty?" He guessed.

"I was twenty three in February and my mother told me that my father died on a motorcycle when I was two and a half." He said pausing. "His name was Phillip Mason and she gave me this picture of him." He added as he reached for his wallet from his pocket. "This was his senior picture that she gave me to keep because she wanted me to know what he looked like." He said a moment later as he showed the worn photograph to Michael.

"Then Miss Barbara is your grandmother." Michael said as he stared intently at the picture. "Man this is a God thing, I don't know what else to call it."

"My mother told me that she got pregnant with me right before they graduated from high school and then he broke up with her a couple of months later." Andre' continued. "But she wanted me to know what he looked like so she gave me this picture."

"So your mother never knew Miss Barbara because they broke up before you were born." Michael said as he tried to get an understanding of the circumstances.

"They broke all the way up, she told me that he didn't try to pay her any support or nothin' like that man."

"She's gonna flip out when she finds this out." Michael said then. "Are you ready to go talk to her and see if this is the real deal?"

"Maybe this is just some kind of bizarre stuff that's not real or somethin.'"

"Do you mind if I take a picture of this and send it to Douglas' phone and ask him if it's the same guy?" Michael suggested then. "If it is, then there's no question about it, she's your grandmother."

"Do what you have to do man, I'm still tryin' to put all of this together." He said as he took the small photo from his wallet for him to snap and send.

He's gonna call when he gets this, watch it." Michael said as he aimed his phone at the picture.

"Is he at work right now?"

"He is but he keeps his phone on, this won't take long, two minutes tops." He added as he sent a text message along with the photo.

"How does this stuff happen?" Andre' asked as he sat staring at the twenty five year old picture of his father.

"This is just me but I think this is God's way of showin' us just how much He cares about the things that we go through." Michael said after thinking a moment. "I've talked to Miss Barbara a couple of times and so has Douglas and we both noticed the same thing about her."

"What?" He asked out of curiosity.

"We know how lonely she is and when she finds out about you, she's gonna fall apart, I already see it."

"How long have you known her?"

"Just a couple of weeks and it was really odd how it happened." Michael began. "She likes to walk around the block and one day I was out there cuttin' the grass and I think she might've been drinkin'." He said laughing a little. "She thought I was Douglas and she started cussin' me out because she said I hadn't come to see her in a while." "I had never seen this woman in my life and then it came to me that she was mistakin' me for him, it was wild."

"She doesn't have any other family or anything?"

"Phillip was all she had and she's really had a hard time with it and it's been twenty years." "And when the light came on in my head that she thought she was talkin' to Douglas, I had to let him know that it had been too long since he had come to see about her.

"Lonely." Andre' said.

"And you know it so when she finds out that she has a grandson that she didn't know about, it's gonna be unreal to her." Michael said as his ringtone sounded.

"That wasn't even two minutes."

"Watch this." Michael said as he put his phone on speaker.

"Are you serious?" Douglas asked him.

"Is that Phillip?" Michael asked him.

"That's him and if you didn't have the Holy Ghost, I would think you were lyin.'"

"Well I do and I'm not."

"Did he call you or how did all of this come up?"

"He's here with me, you can ask him."

"I'm right here and I'm pretty shocked right now." Andre' told him a moment later. "She called him a few minutes ago because she needed some help at her house and somehow, it just all came together." "I'm just in shock."

"I can see why but this is nothin' for you to afraid of because God has done this son."

"Yes sir."

"I don't know your grandmother that well but I do know that you have a real opportunity to be a blessing to her especially since the Lord has saved you and allowed all of this to come out." "This is all for a reason and you might not understand why things have worked out like this but this is when you first start to trust God with your life."

"Yes sir." He said again.

"So when you go over there, it might be a good thing to let her know that you found out some good news this mornin' and if you don't mind, let me know how it goes."

"We should be done twice as fast with two of you here." Barbara remarked ten minutes later as she let Michael and Andre' in the house.

"Miss Barbara, this is Andre', I met him a couple of days ago." Michael told her as he introduced them. "And I think you need to sit down for a minute, we have somethin' to tell you."

"Nobody has died have they?" She asked cautiously.

"No ma'am." Michael said as he encouraged her to sit down.

"We were talkin' this mornin' a few minutes ago and we just found out that you're my grandmother." Andre' said nervously half a minute later as he once again got his wallet out and showed her Phillip's picture.

"Where did you get this?" She asked him as tears began to form in her eyes a few moments later.

"My mother gave me this after she told me about his accident."

"He never told me that he had a baby." She barely got out.

"She told me that they broke up a couple of months after they graduated from high school." He told her. "And I know that it's probably gonna take some time for you to even believe this and if you want to, I can have my mother call you if you need to talk to her." He added as he noticed the look of shock on her face.

She didn't answer but began to study his face, searching for some resemblance of Phillip in him.

"Do you think she would mind?" She finally asked him.

"I don't think she would mind talkin' to you but if you're not ready to do that, we can wait." He told her.

"The accident happened when he was twenty one and you said that they broke up right after they got out of high school?" She asked him as she tried to figure out the timeline.

"Yes ma'am, she said that I was two and a half when it happened so I never knew anything about him."

"Are you okay Miss Barbara?" Michael asked her then as she got up and began to slowly walk around the room in a daze.

"I'm just tryin' to understand why he never told me." She said as she sat back down a moment later. "All of this time, you could've been in my life but he never told me about you." She said with a desperate tone in her voice.

"You don't know why he didn't and there's nothin' that you can do about that but just be glad and thankful that you found out when you did." Michael told her.

"Now you're soundin' exactly like your big brother, he's rubbin' off on you." She said while laughing and crying at the same time. "Does he know about this?"

"I called him and sent that picture to his phone so we would know for sure that that was him." "And he was just as surprised as you are, he ddn't tell him either, as close as they were."

"Do you know Douglas?" She asked Andre'.

"I met him for the first time on Sunday."

"Do you know that he was the last person to see your father alive?" "They were together when the accident happened and that's why I feel a connection to him and you should too." She said as she took his hands into hers. "Do you mind if I give you a hug?" She asked him.

Then without saying another word, he leaned towards her and allowed her to embrace him as he did her in return. It was then that she experienced a release within herself as she openly wept as she was able to somehow connect to a living part of her son, taken in the prime of his life.

17

"I'm sorry if it seems like I can't help myself but you guys have to realize how long it's been since I've actually had somebody that I can call my family." Barbara remarked ten minutes later after she had regained her composure and was able to talk to them.

"You don't have to apologize for that, we understand, so you can call this a new start for both of you." Michael told her. "Do you still feel like dealin' with the boxes?"

"It will just take a few minutes, I promise you guys." She said as she started towards the basement door. "They're right there at the bottom of the stairs."

"Did you pack these up yourself?" Michael asked her a few minutes later after he and Andre' sat the four boxes down for her to sort through.

"No honey, I have no idea what's here and I'm glad that I have you two here with me because I'm a little afraid of what we might find." Barbara admitted. "And Andre', since we know now that Phil was your father, I want you to feel free to take some of his things with you."

He nodded as they watched her slowly and cautiously pull back the packing tape that the first box was sealed with.

"It looks like all that's in this one is a bunch of picture albums." She said a minute later after she counted four neatly stacked one on top of another, along with a high school yearbook.

"Do you mind if I start lookin' through these?" Andre' asked her as he picked up the first album in the stack.

"Not at all, help yourself." "These were your father's things so you have the right." She told him. "And Michael, you too, you might find some pictures of Douglas that you want." She added as she handed him a second album.

"This is a little surreal." Michael said five minutes later after he came across several pictures of Phillip and Douglas sitting in a night club surrounded by barely dressed women, joints and alcohol bottles. "This is not my brother." He added, shaking his head. "And it's one thing to hear about this stuff but when you see pictures like this, it's altogether different."

"And they were tight, you didn't see one without the other one and that's why he took it so hard." Barbara said.

"Do you mind if I look at those?" Andre' asked him.

"Look at these pictures and you'll get a good idea of what the Holy Ghost does for you when you let it work." Michael told him as he handed the album to him.

"Do you think he would mind if I talked to him about my father?"

"There's one way to find out, I'll call him again and tell him that you wanna get together with him and I'll get back with you." Michael said as he picked up another album.

"This is my mother." Andre' said in astonishment a minute later as he found a twenty five year old senior prom photograph of Phillip and his mother, Nancy Turner.

"This is more proof, how crazy is that?" Michael said as he closely examined the picture.

"Would you feel better if we had a D.N.A. test done or somethin'?" "That way we would know a hundred percent that this is true."

"I'm pretty sure that goin' by what we're seein' here and what your mother told you but I can ask you the same thing can't I?" "Would you feel better if we did that?"

"That would be the only way to get rid of any question marks and nobody is sayin' that your mother doesn't know what she's talkin' about." Michael said then.

"I understand but how would you do that?" Barbara asked him.

"I've seen those tests at the drug store so it wouldn't be hard to do but it's up to you two." Michael said. "But I'm gonna call Douglas again and see if he has some time this week to get together with you and I'll let you know what I find out.".…

JUNE 12, FRIDAY

"I'm not gonna call it bizarre because this is somethin' that the Lord has done and that's just not the right word." Douglas remarked

Friday evening at the kitchen table with Michael and Andre' after looking at the D.N.A. results that confirmed Phillip's paternity.

"And when I told my mother about this, she couldn't believe it." Andre' said. "She didn't have any idea that my grandmother was anywhere around. He remarked.

"Did she say anything about wantin' to meet her?"

"Not yet but she did say that she was glad that we found her." He said after a moment. "But I still don't understand how this could happen, it's off the hook crazy."

"It seems that way but there's not anything that God doesn't know about." Douglas said as he continued to read over the test results. "None of this was an accident because of the way everything fell into place and there might be even more comin' out of this."

"Has she noticed anything different about you?" Michael asked Andre'.

"When I went by her place to tell her about this and after I told her how I met my father's old friend at a church, she was just shocked."

"Did she ask you how that happened?"

"She didn't ask and I didn't tell her because I don't want her to ever know how low down I let myself go." He said, shaking his head.

"But the good thing about that son is that all of what happened is gone forever so don't let anybody throw it up in your face; I don't care who it is." Douglas told him. "And I know that it might sound like a stretch, but if none of that had happened, both you and Terry would probably still be out there on the devil's territory but God sees the big picture."

"I didn't think about it like that."

"All of that was a horrible thing on the surface but He knows how to turn things around." He continued. "Salvation and healing came out of it and now that you have what it takes, there's no tellin' what you can do yourself in somebody else's life; that's the way it works."

"I really wish you could've been there when we told Miss Barbara that she has a grandson that she didn't know about." Michael commented. "It was priceless."

"I'm sure it was and the thing about it is, the chances of this happenin' on its own are probably slim to none, but when God gets involved, nothin' is impossible." Douglas said as he handed the paper back to Andre'. "And don't ever lose this, you might need it for legal proof at some point."

Andre' nodded a little before he gathered his thoughts before speaking again.

"Is there somethin' that you're tryin' to say, we've been doin' most of the talkin' man." Michael said.

"I was just wonderin' what he was like and all of that stuff." He finally said after a moment. "And if it bothers you to talk about him I understand but you're the only person that I know that actually knew him besides my mother."

"Have you had a chance to ask her about him yet?"

"She doesn't like to talk about him, the only thing she's ever told me was the way he died and she gave me his senior picture to keep so I would know what he looked like."

"He was the type of person that liked to keep you jokin' and laughin' all of the time." Douglas said as he reflected back to the few years of their friendship. "And that might be why we were able to stick, we cancelled each other out; I was the one that was as mean as a junkyard dog and he was just the opposite."

"That's how you got that name huh?" Michael asked him.

"I don't know who started that but I still see some of those same people that I used to run with and that's the first thing I hear, what's goin' on Junkyard." Douglas said.

"They won't let you live it down huh?"

"Did you tell him about those pictures that we found the other day?' Andre' asked Michael then.

"They're out in the car, I didn't know if you wanted to go there or not so I didn't bring 'em in."

"That depends on what they're pictures of." He said after a moment. "And I think you know where not to go Michael Johnson."

"I really do appreciate you and Michael takin' up tme like this with me because I didn't have any idea what was goin' on 'til he started breakin' stuff down to me." Andre' said after Michael went out to his car for the pictures.

"When this happened to us, we probably didn't know much more than you do and somebody had to do the same thing with me so don't ever feel like you're in the way or anything even close to that." Douglas told him. "There are things that you have to be taught because if you're not, you can find yourself right back out there where you came from and I really don't think that's what you want."

"It's not." He said, shaking his head a little.

"And because you're startin' to live such a different way than what you're used to, it's a matter of allowin' your gift of the Holy Ghost to lead you."

"And I couldn't believe some of those pictures that Michael showed me the other day but it's helpin' me to see that this is more than a lot of talk."

"I'm not sure what he's about to show me but it can't be anything good." He admitted. "But once you get to the place where you know how to use what God has given you, you won't recognize yourself."

"It's already startin' to be like that." He began. "This time last week, I already been to the liquor store stockin' up for the week-end and it's unreal how I haven't even thought about goin' there." "The taste for it is just gone, it's crazy man."

"But it's real and you don't realize how bad off you were until look back at yourself and actually see the damage that the world can do to you." He told him. "You don't see it because it happens little by little and before you know it, you're so far out there that it takes more to make you come to yourself."

"Do you mean that things happen to you to let you know how much help you need?"

"In a nutshell, you're exactly right son." Douglas remarked. "And with me, it was the way that I saw your father die right in front of me; it was enough to blow my mind to the point where I almost took myself out but God had other plans." "Just like what happened to you on Sunday, the Lord stepped in and did what He does best." "He saves souls and you have His power now to help other people by tellin' what He did for you."

Andre' nodded then with understanding as he began to remember the words of Terry's testimony that had caused him to believe what God would do.

"And one of the sweetest things about this salvation is once you've taken on the name of Jesus through water baptism, and then receive His spirit because you found a place of repentance, you're justified." He said as he paused for a brief moment. "And what I mean by that is all of the dirt and mess that we got involved in out there is gone and wiped out like those things never happened and if that's not enough to send you to the moon and back, I don't know what is."

"That's some deep stuff right there man." He said as he began to process what he had just ministered to him.

"It is but at the same time, it's not so deep that we can't understand it, you know what I mean?" Douglas asked him. "When you think about that kind of love and the power in the name of Jesus that cleans us up, it's a little too much sometimes."

"When you said that about not understandin' it, I had no idea this was about to happen to me on Sunday. He began. "But when she started talkin' about feelin' like a kid on Christmas mornin' right before she went down in that water, that's what got me up out of my seat on the back row." He said as tears began to run down his face. "Somethin' like clicked in me and made me go up there to talk to her and you know the rest."

"It was powerful and I know for a fact that she didn't understand altogether what was happenein' to her either but she believed it and that's what the Lord is lookin' for." "He didn't tell us to understand everything that He tells us but when you believe it anyway, that's when He'll do what He promised to." "That's how she got over, she saw how different Michael was from what he was down in St. Louis and that had a lot to do with it too." Douglas said. "And always remember, it's not so much what you say to people that makes a difference because anybody can talk a big game but when you get down to business and start livin' your life totally opposite from what you're used to,somebody's gonna notice it."

"Man I was lookin' at some of these pictures we found and I couldn't believe it." Andre' said as Michael came back up.

"Did he put dates on these?" Douglas asked a minute later as he turned the photos over one by one after taking taking quick glimpses of his former self which caused him to experience a flood of mixed emotions.

"He didn't but those are probably twenty one or two years old aren't they?" Michael asked him.

"Somewhere in there and when I look at these, it just makes me that much more thankful for what the Lord delivered me from." "And you have to move on from stuff like this but at the same time, He doesn't want you to forget about how different things could've been." Douglas concluded as he was obviously moved by the images of the years before.

"So it was right after the accident that you started to get it together?" Andre' asked him as he attempted to get a clear understanding of his story.

"It was a major wake up call and it took a week for me to get it." Douglas said in retrospect. "I couldn't eat or sleep and it got to the place where I was at my breakin' point." "That was somethin' that I wasn't used to because Junkyard didn't take down for anybody or anything but I found out quick that my arms were too short to box with God and when you get to that place, that's when things happen for you."

"And you didn't know anything about what to do?" Andre' asked him, totally fascinated.

"Had no clue but Irene got on the phone and called her mother because she didn't know what to do with me, I was a hot mess as the kids say." He said as he clearly remembered the night. "It was a Saturday night, exactly a week after the accident and she got on the phone and told me to come to church the next day and to let God help me." "Didn't really wanna hear anything like that but I was too worn out to argue with her."

24

"And that's one lady that you don't argue with, I found that out too." Michael said.

"She knows what the power of God can do but don't misunderstand me." Douglas said. "The Lord isn't gonna force Himself on anybody or get you in a headlock and make you do anything." "He gives you a choice but if you care about where your soul spends Eternity, it's really a no brainer." "Hell is too hot and Heaven is too wonderful for words and whatever we have to go through to get there, can't even be compared."

"Man when you put it like that, it is a no brainer." Andre' said, agreeing with him.

"It is and don't be afraid to tell people what God has done for you because that's how He draws people." "Everybody doesn't care but you never know whose life you're affecting just by your testimony."

"I know that I hadn't gone to hear what Terry had to say, I wouldn't have a clue so that's my proof." Andre' said as he thought back to Sunday's experience.

"And I'll tell you the same thing that I told her." Douglas said. "If the opportunity comes up for you to talk to somebody, just tell about what happened to you without tryin' to get deep with a lot of scriptures that you don't know enough about yet." "Nobody can ever take your testimony away and sometimes that's more effective than a hundred scriptures that you can try to quote without really knowin' what you're talkin' about.

"I don't have as much to say as she did but anything is better than nothin' at all."

"But sometimes less is better and I'm not takin' anything away from what she had to say because evidently, it did what it was supposed to do." Douglas remarked. "My Lord, what a mess." He added as he came across a picture of himself standing outside a strip club.

"If you don't wanna see anymore of these man, just say the word." Michael told him as he noticed his expressions of distaste at the images that were over twenty years old.

"It is what it is but for some reason, I'm startin' to think that there's some unfinished business goin' on here." He commented as he continued to quickly go through the album. "And Andre', I didn't come across your grandmother by accident so there might be somethin' that I haven't dealt with after all of this time."

"Do you mean between you two?" Andre' asked him.

"I don't know what that could be but she surfaced out of nowhere and then when you come through on top of it, there's some kind of issue goin' on." He said as he closed the album after seeing more than enough reminders of his "Junkyard" days.

"I just had a thought and if you don't think it's a good idea, I'll understand." Michael said after a moment.

"Let's hear it."

"Did she go through these albums and pick out the pictures that she wanted?" Michael asked Andre'.

"I went back over there yesterday and she told me that she had everything she wanted from those boxes that we brought up so I think she's done with everything."

"Why don't you burn all those up and you'll never have to look at 'em again." Michael suggested then.

"That's probably a pretty good idea, that was then and this is now."...

CHAPTER 2

JUNE 14, SUNDAY

"When we first moved out here it took a couple of days to get used to how quiet it is but you can't pay me to go back now." Frances remarked as she and Jane made submarine sandwiches for dinner Sunday afternoon.

"The first mornin' we woke up out here I thought maybe I was dreamin' or somethin', no kiddin." "And some of the kids are gettin' lost in here, it's crazy but it's a good thing at the same time."

"Has your mother been out here since you moved in?"

"Not yet but I talked to her last night and let her know that everybody comes out here on Sunday and if she wants to come it's okay but she hasn't been out here in a couple of weeks."

"Does she have a reason for that?"

"She hasn't actually said so but I think she's havin' a real problem with Chris and James and the money that she gave him."

"He told me about that little incident and I think he still feels a little condemned about the way he did it but what's done is done."

"She would've found it out anyway and he didn't have any reason to be holdin' that back and he doesn't have anything to apologize for." Jane said, becoming irritated.

"Honey it's okay, don't let things like that take your peace of mind." Frances told her.

"I won't but sometimes if I think about it too much, it's enough to take you places where you shouldn't be." She said as she opened a jar of pickles. "I talked to him about it a couple of weeks ago and he's really havin' a hard time with it because it's startin' to affect the kids a little, you know what I mean?"

"Chris told me about what happened at this new school they're goin' to this fall but like I told her, this is just the beginnin' so don't be surprised when you see it over and over again."

"She said she can't even take her to the store without people starin' at her and Patti like they're from outer space and it's really irritating to him."

"And I can remember sittin' them down when they got engaged and lettin' them know that racism is still alive and remains so there's always gonna be somethin' to test 'em, you know that."

Yes ma'am I do but it seems to be worse now than it used to be."

"But that's like anything else, things aren't gonna get any better so what you have to do is step up and make the difference even when it doesn't seem to make any sense."

"Liz told me the other day that my mother told her to be careful who she picks to be friends with and she wanted to know what she meant by that." Jane said. "And I know exactly what she meant, she wants all of her friends to be white and she's havin' a problem with that."

"How old is she, twelve or thirteen?" "I can't keep up with all of their ages, you're gonna have to help me out with that."

"She's thirteen and about to go to middle school and after hearin' about what Paul has had to deal with, it's nothin' like it was when I was that age." Jane commented.

"But they know right from wrong, I really don't think you're gonna have that much of a problem."

"I hope not because peer pressure can shoot that out of the water mom." She said. "And that's one of the reasons why they can't do Facebook and all of that 'til they're eighteen and they know better than to try it because Paul would find out and they don't wanna go there."

"They might get upset about that but like I heard Chris tell Stephen the other day when he got a little attitude about havin' to clean up the bathroom the other day."

"What did she tell him, I can just see and hear that one." Jane said, laughing at her.

"James made up a job chart for them to follow and he hung it up in the kitchen and every last one of 'em except Byron has somethin' to do." She continued.

"I like that idea, I might have to come over there and check that out." "But what happened?"

"He marked his name off the chart and when Chris went to check behind him, all he did was change the toilet paper roll and he thought that was all he had to do." She said. "So she went in his room and took his video game out of his hands and walked him into the bathroom and told him to show her what he had done."

"You can't play with these kids because they'll try anything if you don't watch 'em."

"And they're findin' that out, he told her that it wasn't fair for him to have that job and she told him that life wasn't fair and he needed to get over it and get busy."

"It's really too bad that we have to talk to 'em like that but they have this spirit that's drivin' them to say and do things that we wouldn't have even thought about."

"And that's why you have to pray over 'em every day and keep 'em goin' to Sunday school as much as it might seem like it's not makin' a difference."

"They already know, they don't have a choice when it comes to that."

"And it's not that you're forcin' anything on 'em but you're obligated to train 'em up in the right way so they won't have any excuses later on." Frances said. "When Irene was out there doin' her thing with Douglas, I had the comfort in my spirit that even though it seemed like I had lost her, she knew what was right and she wasn't gonna forget it, no matter how bad it looked on the surface."

"I remember how much she hated my guts and at the time I just couldn't understand what the problem was, I was crazy about Paul, I thought that was all that mattered."

"It should've been but you have to remember that she was runnin' with people that encouraged division and hatred." Frances said. "And even though I didn't bring them up to think like that, she was tryin' to prove a point to me that she was gonna think for herself, no matter what I thought about it."

"That's what my mother said I was doin', she thought I was goin' through a phase with church and Paul and all of that; they thought that I was gonna graduate from college and find a job that would pay me a six figure salary and the whole nine yards but the Lord had other plans."

"Have I ever told you how proud I am of you and Paul for the way you're raisin' all of these kids like you are?"

"You don't have to, I think we know it."

"But it never hurts to hear it anyway because I know you've heard a lot of negative stuff about why you have so many kids but as long as you're not askin' anybody to help you, I don't know what the problem is."

"It's because most people don't understand how we're doin' it without public assistance and stuff like that but when you're trustin' God, it's not hard and I don't have to tell you that."

"You don't but doin' things that way seems like craziness to anybody that doesn't know God and that's why you have to be so patient with people." "If a person hasn't been taught, you can't expect that much." Frances added as she finished making another sandwich.

"Did I ever tell you about the time I made a pot of chili with one pound of hamburger and there was enough of it left for the next day?"

"Honey I've seen that happen so many times that I can't count." Frances remarked. "I didn't have a choice but to trust God and I think sometimes that's where He wants us so He can prove Himself."

"Douglas told me probably two or three years ago that we need to remember that this is the same God that parted the Red Sea and we can't put Him in a box like He's limited." She said. "I never have forgotten that and it's helped me through some rough times."

"And this is the same man that would curse you out for lookin' at him the wrong way." Frances said. "That should show anybody how powerful He is."

"I don't even remember what we were talkin' about but that makes so much sense."

"It makes sense because God doesn't change, just because that was thousands of years ago doesn't mean anything and if you have enough faith to ask Him to do things that seem impossible, that's when impossible things happen." She said as Michael and Terry walked in.

"Say that again, I like the way that sounded." Michael said as he came over to hug her.

"Did that sound good to you?" She asked him.

"It sounded good to me too, I wanna hear some more." Terry said "And this is so nice, you're probably feelin' like you're in another world don't you?" She asked Jane as she looked around.

"That's a good way to put it honey, when you go from fifteen hundred square feet to almost four thousand, that's a big difference."

"Are you gonna take me on a tour, this feels like somethin' that you could charge admission to see." She said.

"Did Michael tell you that he painted all of these rooms by himself?" Jane asked her as they started out of the kitchen a minute later.

"He told me that he was helpin' out here but he didn't tell me that." Terry said surprised. "He did a good job didn't he?" She said as they walked down a hallway towards the girl's bedrooms.

"He really did, I think he took it on as a challenge and you can't tell that this was his first project." Jane said. "He would come out here by himself after workin' all night to get it done so he was serious." She added as they turned the corner.

"So you have all of the girls over here and the boys on the other side over there?" Terry asked.

"You got it and they love it like that." "Before we moved we had 'em separated in four bedrooms but they're growin' up and that wasn't workin' anymore." "So altogether, there's eight bedrooms, four on this side and four on the other and they're lovin' it because they can spread out now."

"Is it nine boys and ten girls or the other way around?" Terry asked becoming fascinated by the organization and order of the household. "Irene told me the way it was but I forgot which is which."

"That's it, nine and ten and my mother thinks we're crazy but it is what it is." Jane said. "And after the sextuplets were born, everybody thought we were done but it didn't work out that way."

"Is it because of Paul that she's havin' a problem or is it because of the number of kids that you have?"

"It's a combination of the two, she can't stand the thought of him havin' control as she likes to say." She said. "She's livin' in the past where this just wasn't done and if it was, you were breakin' the law."

"Are you serious?"

"That sounds unreal now but that's the way it was in the generation that she grew up in and it's been a fight from the beginnin' with her." Jane remarked. "And believe it or not, there's still some churches that believe in that segregation stuff and that doesn't make it any easier when you're tryin' to go there with her."

"Has she ever been to church with you?"

"The day we got married was the first and last time that she was there and she had to make herself show up that day." "And I had to find somebody else to give me away because my father wasn't gonna have anything to do with it, that's how bitter he was."

"So why didn't all of that make you the same way?"

"I'm not really sure but she thought that just because they were that way, I would automatically be like them and when it didn't work out that way, they were pretty much in a state of shock." Jane said. "And I don't know how we got off into all of that, I'm supposed to be takin' you on a tour." She added as they slowly walked down the girl's hallway.

"We were talkin' about Paul and your mother but it's funny how she decided to do all of this after givin' you a hard time about it before."

"It was one of those things that come out of nowhere, we had started talkin' about findin' a bigger place and I hadn't said anything to her at all." Jane said as they turned into one of the rooms and sat down on a bed. "But when you're doin' the right thing the Lord will see to it that you get what you need, even before you ask Him for it because He already knows."

"That is so good to know and every time I get to talk to somebody, I find out somethin' new that's really helpin' me."

"Just make sure that you're talkin' to people that have been around for a while and can tell you how to make it through some things."

"Like Douglas and Aunt Frances."

"You got it honey, I used to talk to your brother and come away feelin' like I could go just a little bit farther." Jane said in retrospect.

"Really?" Terry asked, surprised.

She nodded. "Yes ma'am, he would tell me things that would help me keep stuff in perspective and when James' mother turned on him because of Chris, that's when he stepped up and helped him stay afloat."

"That's somethin' else that Irene told me about, she said that's why they're so tight now."

"It is and Douglas might've been a lot of things out there when he was Junkyard but racism was never his thing."

"Do you think he could help your mother out?" Terry asked, half seriously.

"He'd probably be glad to talk to her but if you don't think you have a problem, you can't be helped unless the Lord does it." "He could put some things on her mind but when you've been one way for so long, it takes God to rock your world."

"Don't I know it and when I think about myself just a couple of months ago, I could almost throw up."

"So are you still tellin' people about what happened tp you?"

"Every time I hear somebody say that I look different from what I used to, I have to and it's mostly customers that come in the store." She said. "I had one guy tell me that my face was glowin' and I'm like, what?"

"What it is, is that other people can see the joy that you have now that was missin' before and I don't care what anybody says, this is more real than what we realize so don't ever lose that."

"There's no way, because for one thing, if I would start to let myself go back to what I was, too many people would be sayin' I told you so."

"And they're watchin' to see if you really have what you say you do." "Have you been back down to St. Louis since all of this happened to you?"

"I'm finally about to get my car and Michael's goin' down there with me for a couple of days and I already know what that'll be like."

"Just be yourself and don't try to make anybody believe anything, your life says it all.

"I called her yesterday and told her what Chris came up with about her movin' here to an assisted livin' place." Janice remarked as she and Michael walked down the road after dinner an hour later.

"So what did she have to say about that?"

"She was surprised and I don't think she thought it was a good idea until I told her that she'd be able to see the baby any time she wanted to." Janice said as he took her hand.

"Aren't you pretty close to half way done?"

"I'm like twenty three weeks and a couple of days, somethin' like that." "I have a calendar up in my room and her due date is marked on it and it's startin' to get a little scary."

"And when is Chris due?"

"She's not due until January and she told me the other day that she was jealous because I have just three months left." Janice remarked. "But she doesn't have to go through what I'm about to, it's not gonna be much fun doin' this by myself but it is what it is."

"Who said you're doin' it by yourself, you have too many people around here that aren't gonna let you do that."

"This is on me and I don't think anybody else should have to pay for what I let happen, you know what I mean?"

"Are you still beatin' yourself up about that?"

"Not really but this baby is gonna be a fact of my life so I'm tryin' to get my mind ready for what's comin' Michael." She insisted.

"You're not sorry that you didn't go the other way are you?"

"I'm not and I still think about the night Douglas told me that that wasn't an option." She said in reflection. "And he didn't know me like that but it really meant somethin' to have somebody care enough to tell me what was right."

"And it's been like that ever since huh?"

"It has but I don't want him to feel like that I'm gonna be runnin' to him every time I have a problem either, that's what prayer is for." She said, laughing a little.

"But there's two ways to look at that, you can pray about somethin' and you can get your answer from the person that the Lord put in your life." Michael said after thinking a moment. "Like I can be thinkin' and wonderin' about some kind of issue and Aunt Frances can come up with the right solution almost every time." "And she always takes me to a couple of scriptures that'll hit me right where it counts, I'm not kiddin'."

"And she's probably the one that helped get him goin' in the right direction; they think just alike." Janice commented. "If you ask them the same question, you'd probably get identical answers and I might do that just for the fun of it."

"What would you ask 'em?"

"I have to think about that but by next week, I'm gonna try it and see what happens."

"I want you to let me know if you start feelin' tired, then we can turn around and head back." Michael told her then.

"Are you ready to get wet, 'Nita's gettin' a water balloon fight together for the kids."

"I'm stayin' out of that because I know she'll do it." Michael said. "I've never met anybody as bold as she is and you can't get mad at her because she does crazy stuff that makes you laugh."

"Sheila said that her and Ruth used to be the same way, then after the night that she got shot, that was their wake up call."

"Hold up, Sheila never told me about that."

"It happened five or six years ago when they went up to Dubuque with James to see his sister one night." She began. "They think that whoever did it saw them in the car with him and didn't like it and she got shot in the neck and almost didn't make it."

"So that's what that scar on her neck is from?" "I noticed it one day but I didn't think it was any of my business to ask her about it."

"That's where that came from and she might tell you about it if you ask her to." Janice said as they continued to walk.

"She's really got a testimony, that can take you out in a second." "I worked with a dude that got it in the neck one night and he was gone before he hit the ground." "It was one of those drive-by shootings where he was in the wrong place at the wrong time."

"It's because of things like that that Aunt Frances tells me not to leave the house before prayin' first because it's so crazy out here."

"And you know it and since it is so wild, I think we need to have a conversation."

"I know we do and if you didn't bring it up, I was goin' to." Janice said as if reading his mind.

"So what are you thinkin'?"

"I'm thinkin' that we need to talk about what we're doin'." She said after a moment. "And I don't wanna take anything for granted and think it's gonna be one way and you're thinkin' somethin' else altogether."

"Is that the way I'm comin' off to you?" "If I am, let me know and I'll make sure that I put a stop to it."

"It's not you, it's me and my problem of not bein' able to let myself go ahead and believe that this'll work for us."

"And it's the baby that's puttin' doubts in your mind isn't it?"

She nodded a little in agreement. "And if you put yourself in my place, it might be easier for you to understand why I'm bein' so careful." She added as she began to let her emotions show. "I mean her own father doesn't want to have anything to do with her so

36

why should I think that you're just gonna take over somebody else's responsibility when you don't have to Michael."

"I totally understand where you're comin' from because like Douglas tells me all of the time, talk is so cheap that you're better off with a penny to spend because it can be pretty worthless." Michael responded with patient sensitivity. "But the thing about that is, I can't prove myself to you until she's born and I don't blame you a bit for bein' skeptical Janice.

"She nodded again as she continued to listen to him with appreciation for his apparent effort to reassure her of his intentions.

"And the number one thing that's even more important is the fact that you belong to the Lord and I don't have time to be playin' with your emotions and gettin' in trouble with God." He added. "Aunt Frances got me straight about that from the beginnin' and you don't know how glad I am to have people like her and Douglas and James that aren't afraid to tell you the truth about things, whether you wanna hear it or not."

"I know, sometimes it hurts when you hear it but if it changes you and makes you do stuff different, I guess it's worth it."

"It is, but back to us, and if you're okay with this, maybe we should agree to keep goin' like we're doin, and when the baby gets here, we'll see what happens." Michael suggested to her. "And when I say that, it doesn't mean there's a chance that I'm gonna change my mind about you just because you have a baby." "I noticed that the first time I saw you and I'd really like to see you make it easier on yourself by not worryin' about that."

"I'm tryin'not to and I really love how patient you're bein' with me but I think you're right when you say we'll wait and see what happens." Janice said then. "It wouldn't be fair to you for me to hold you to anything, it's just too soon."

"But I think we're gettin' there and the last time I talked to James, he told me about the fifth chapter of Ephesians." He said as he noticed a deer on the right side of the road and guided Janice away from it. "Maybe we need to start back." He told her as they slowed down.

"He was cute, get a picture of him." She suggested.

"Do you really want me to?" He asked as he took his phone from his shirt pocket.

"If you can get it before he runs away, send it to my phone and I'll print it off and frame it."

"If it means that much to you I'm goin' for it." He said as he aimed his phone and quickly took the picture before the deer ran off.

"I'm startin' to try to get the nursery together and that might be somethin' I'll use if it comes out okay."

"Then you'll be able to say that I had somethin' to do with it." Michael said as they turned back around and headed back in the opposite direction.

"So what were you about to say about Ephesians five?" She asked him then.

"Yeah, thanks for remindin' me." Michael began. "James told me that that's a good chapter to read for anybody that thinks they're ready to get married." He said as he began to search for the bible app on his phone. "And when he put it like that, I went there and read it and found out what he meant."

"I haven't gotten there yet, what does it say?"

"Basically that if you're married, you have to have the same kind of love for each other that the Lord has for the church and that's a lot of love." He said, shaking his head a little.

"It is but you know that it can be done because both of us see it every day." Janice said. "I've been watchin' Chris and James ever since I got here and sometimes I can't believe the difference from what I was used to seein' when I was growin' up."

"Like how, you don't mind me askin' do you?"

"I don't mind because it is what it is." "I don't think they had any real feelings for each other because they were always into it about somethin' and most of the time it was over petty nothin' stuff."

"So you never saw them act like they ever cared about each other?"

She shook her head after thinking a moment. "I can remember Marie and me thinkin' that they were arguin' about us because we heard it every day." She said. "And that's all I knew, then when I came here and saw just the opposite, it was like I couldn't believe what I was seein.'"

"I asked James one time if he ever felt like he was walkin' on egg shells because of the race thing."

"What did he say, that's sort of interestin' when you think about it."

"He said they might've had some issues at first but they're over that stuff." Michael remarked. "And they give me ammunition for people that want to say that marriage is outdated and not happenin' anymore."

"Do you hear that a lot?"

"I hear it a lot at work and it's like if you get married, you're strange or crazy and that just makes me more thankful that the Lord is savin' me from that kind of thinkin' because it's everywhere."

"I know it is, I have to listen to it on my job too and I just stopped sayin' anything because nobody cares what I think anyway." Janice said. "And I was startin' to sort of feel like I was the one that was strange 'til Aunt Frances sat me down one day and had me read that verse in Hebrews somewhere."

"Do you remember what it said?"

"She had me read it out loud like she wanted to make sure that I got it, and what I remember the most about it was where it said that marriage is honorable in all and I forget the rest but that stuck with me."

"That's what Google is for, I'm lookin' that one up before we get back." Michael said. "That sounded good." He added while slowing down to type on his phone.

"And I had no idea that was in there until she showed me but it made me feel like I have some back up, you know what I mean?"

"It makes sense now but if you had told me this same thing six months ago I might've laughed in your face." Michael remarked as he continued to search for the scripture.

"I know I would have and that's why I don't try to make people understand stuff like that because you really can't 'til you have the Holy Ghost." Janice said. "Did you find it?"

"I think so, Hebrews thirteen and four?" "Does that sound right?"

"What does it say?"

"Marriage is honorable in all and the bed undefiled then it starts talkin' about whores and adultery." He added, starting to laugh. "I love it."

"It's just all in there and I don't know how I was makin' it before but I guess you don't know any better 'til your eyes come open."

"Like you don't miss what you've never had?"

"Somethin' like that and I've thought about tryin' to talk to my mother about it but I think she'd try to shut me down as soon as I would even start to go there."

"She might not, don't let that stop you."

"If it comes up some kind of way, I wouldn't have any problem lettin' her know about what I know is right and I think she knows too but just doesn't wanna do anything about it."

"Sort of like 'Nita?"

"Exactly like 'Nita and we talk about it all of the time but when you're hung up on what other people are doin' or not doin', it's like that's her excuse, you know what I mean?"

"So what do you tell her?"

"The last time it came up was last week after we got back from Terry's testimony service." Janice began. "And she asked me later on after everybody left why we make so much out of somebody recievin' the Holy Ghost." "She heard us talkin' about Andre' and it was like what's the big deal?"

"It all goes back to not understandin' until it happens to you so really all you can do is be patient with her." "Me and Terry were the same way so I know where she's comin' from." "It takes different things for everybody."

"I wasn't planning on coming out here until one day next week but I need to talk to you now." Jane's mother remarked two hours later with her in the kitchen.

"What's goin' on, you look like you've have a bad day." Jane told her as she sat down at the island.

"I went to the doctor Friday and got some bad news." She began. "I don't want you be stressed out or worried because you have too much else to do." She added as she nervously fumbled with a paper napkin.

"What did you find out?" Jane cautiously asked her.

"I went to the doctor because I've been having this cough that I can't get rid of and they took some X-rays and I have stage three lung cancer." She managed to say. "And I don't understand why this is happening to me, I've been a good person- She said, unable to finish speaking her thoughts because of the feelings of self pity that were overtaking her.

"Mom that doesn't have anything to do with it, things happen whether you think you're all that or not." Jane told her then. "They're not sayin' that you're terminal or anything like that are they?"

"They started talking about chemo or radiation and all of that but I don't have time to be going through all of that Jane." "I'm only sixty eight years old and there's so much more that I want to do and see." She added as she continued to unload her thoughts and fears to her.

"Then I'll tell you what, we're not gonna sit around and wait for things to change." Jane said as she stood up, and came to her side before leading her out of the house and heading towards James and Chris' house, five hundred steps away.

"You didn't let anybody know that we were coming over here Jane, can we do that?" She asked weakly as they approached the house.

"Mom this is my family, this is what we do." Jane said as she slowed down. "And after what you just told me, I can't just sit back and do nothin' about it which is why we're comin' over here."

"Why are we coming over here, I don't understand." She admitted.

"You've never met Paul's mother have you?" Jane asked her then.

"I might have at your wedding but that was so long ago that I don't remember."

"Then that's about to change."

"Is Paul over here too?"

"He's here with the kids, they're havin' a water balloon thing goin' on back there and they'll be happy to see you." Jane told her. "So try to relax a little, you're gonna be alright." She added with an air of certain faith that pleases God.

"So this is the lady that the Lord used to make all of this possible?" Frances asked five minutes later in the family room after Jane introduced them.

"You moved out here with your daughter and James too?" "I didn't know that." Florence said as she slowly sat down on the sofa with her.

"I did and I couldn't be happier out here, it's another world and they really appreciate how everything came together."

"Are Douglas and Irene still here?" Jane asked her.

"They are, Douglas is in the kitchen with James and Randy and I think Irene's with Chris and 'Nita supervisin' all of those balloons out there." She said as she noticed her concerned demeanor.

"I'll be right back." She said as she left the two of them alone.

"What's goin' on hon?" Douglas asked her a few minutes later in the livingroom after she motioned him out of the kitchen.

"My mother just dropped a bomb on me a few minutes ago and somehow we ended up over here." She said before taking a deep breath and sitting down in a nearby chair.

"It doesn't have anything to do with James does it?" He asked her after a moment.

"She shook her head." "That's pretty much nothin' after what I just found out." She began. "She just told me she has stage three lung cancer."

"And?" You know why you ended up over here don't you?" He asked her. "I don't think we have much of a choice but to do what we have to do." "Did you say she's here with you?"

"She's in there with mother and I don't know if my mom feels comfortable enough with her to tell her what's goin' on, but I know that she knows how to help her out, you know what I mean?"

"We both know but my question to you is, how willin' is she to let us call that stuff out of her?"

"She has no idea what the name of Jesus will do Douglas, she's clueless, and all of the talkin' for years that I have done hasn't seem to make a bit of difference to her." Jane said. "And we were just talkin' about how this is the same God that parted the Red Sea, do you remember tellin' me that a couple of years ago?" She asked him as she wiped tears from her face.

"I do and it's as true now as it was then but because she hasn't had to trust and believe God for anything like this before now, she hasn't been able to relate to much you've tried to tell her. He told her. "Any time you can hand somebody a check for twenty-five thousand dollars and not miss it, you don't have any reason to feel like you have to believe on the name of Jesus." "People like us that know what it feels like not to be able to pay your bills haven't had a choice but to trust God for any and everything."

"You're right about that and it's really pretty sad when you think about it."

"But the Lord has a way of gettin' your attention whether you have it like that or not so don't beat up on yourself because it might seem like you haven't had any influence on her."

"I know her Douglas, she's not the type to admit anything like that but it is what it is and I don't want to see her go through any more than she has to."

"Of course you don't, c'mon, we've done enough talkin'." He said as he motioned for her to follow him out.

"I knew it would be just a matter of time before you came in here." Frances said half a minute later as they walked in. "This is my son-in-law Douglas and I don't know if Jane has ever mentioned him to you but we're here to get rid of this problem in the name of Jesus." She added with faith and authority as he sat down on the other side of her.

"I know this is the first time you've laid eyes on me but do you mind tellin' me what you're thinkin' about right now?" He gently and quietly asked her.

"I'm sick." She managed to say. "I'm thinking about how sick I am."

"When did you find this out?"

"I went to the doctor on Friday, they did a chest X-ray and found four or five tumors on my lungs."

"So what's their plan, did they give you any details about what's next for you?" He persisted.

"They're working on my treatment plan and when I go back later next week, I'm supposed to know exactly what they come up with." She said as she began to tremble in fear before Frances reached over and put an arm around her.

"And I understand all of that but can you tell me one more thing?" Douglas asked her as he followed the leading of the Holy Ghost.

She nodded as she gradually began to feel comfortable with him.

"Do you feel like you have enough faith in God for Him to heal you of what they say you have?"

"I've never heard of God doing anything like that." She reluctantly admitted.

"Then can you tell me what that cross you're wearin' means to you?" He asked her, referring to her necklace.

"This means that I believe in God." She said after thinking a moment.

"Then if you believe in God, then you have to know that there's nothin' too big or hard for Him to do." He told her in an attempt to build her faith.

"And we understand that you may not believe like that but we do, so if you don't mind, we're gonna take the time to ask the Lord to take this affliction out of your body." Frances said as she handed Douglas her small bottle of oil from the end table drawer next to her.

She nodded again as she looked over at Jane as if to get her permission and approval after he applied a small amount on her forehead.

"Mom it's okay, nothin' strange is gonna happen so just let us do what she just said." Jane spoke as she came over to her and stood between Douglas and Frances as he quietly began to thank God for the power and authority in the name of Jesus, given through the gift of the Holy Ghost. Then as they began to offer up intercessory faith filled prayer in her behalf, she suddenly screamed out in reaction to the anointing of His touch through their hands that she was experiencing for the first time.

As Frances and Jane held her closer to them, Douglas ended the brief but effective prayer by thanking God for the good report that would be the result of their faith.

"Do you have any idea what you just felt?" Douglas asked her as she sat there feeling dazed at what she had just experienced.

"I know that it was real and I've never felt anything like it before in my life." She expressed as her voice wavered.

"And when we hear back from you that God did the work, it'll be even more real to you." Frances told her.

"But I don't understand why this happened to me or where it came from." She insisted. "I've never smoked or anything like that."

"It doesn't really matter where it came from but it's where it's goin' ma'am and that's what we have to believe." Douglas told her. "Faith is what causes God to work like nothin' else will and if you've ever read about the people that Jesus healed when He was here, it was their faith that got the results." He added. "And I think this is where we're gonna leave it for right now and let God do the rest."...

JUNE 16, TUESDAY

"Girl the last time I saw you, you were barely walkin' and you're drivin' up here in front of my house in a new car?" Doris remarked Tuesday afternoon in St. Louis after Terry and Michael pulled up in her driveway.

"It's been exactly a month and it's almost like all of that never happened." Terry remarked after hugging her.

"Didn't I tell you?" Michael asked her as they started into the house.

"Hold on, hold on, sit down here and talk to me." She said as she led them to her dining room table.

"You've done a lot in here, this looks good." Terry said as she looked around.

"You haven't been in here since the day I moved so it's come a long way in three months." Doris said as she opened the oven for their lunch that she had prepared. "So have you done anything else to your place Michael?"

"I've gotten a couple of rooms painted but I'm takin' my time with that, there's no reason to rush anything." He said as he checked his phone messages.

"You probably don't wanna do a lot of stuff and then have Janice come in there and change stuff huh?"

"We'll see what happens with that." He said with purposeful reservation.

"You're still friends aren't you?"

"Without a doubt but we're still takin' things slow because there's a baby comin' and she wants to be sure about some stuff before we go any farther." Michaels said. "And I see where she's comin' from so I'm not puttin' any kind of pressure on her about anything, I'm learnin' how to wait on things."

"You know that David thinks you're crazy don't you?" She asked him as she sat a platter of fried chicken on the table.

"I know he does and that's his problem." Michael remarked. "If he wants to make himself miserable worryin' about what I'm doin' or not doin', I really can't do anything about that." "I can do a lot of prayin' because that's how I get over but I can't waste my time tryin' to convince him of anything."

"I'll give him the message." She said, laughing at his response.

"I'm serious, I'm findin' out how to come out on top by keepin' my mouth shut and lettin' the Lord fight my battles but at the same time, I know how to defend myself if I have to."

"And I never thought I would hear you talkin' like that guy." She told him. "That tells me Douglas is rubbin' off on you big time." She added as she brought more food over to the table.

"Is that a bad or a good thing?"

"If it's workin' for you then it's a good thing but don't let that stop you from thinkin' for yourself." Doris told him as she sat down. "And I'm comin' back to that because I have to hear about how you can come in here and look like somebody waved a magic wand over you." She told Terry.

"Are you serious?" She asked as she glanced over at Michael.

"Have you been goin' to any counselling or anything?" She asked.

She shook her head. "Why would I waste that kind of money when I don't really need all of that?" She asked as she put baked beans on her plate.

"So you're tellin' me that after all of that that you went through, you're over it just like that?" "Do you know how close they came to killin' you honey?"

"I know they did and sometimes all of that tries to come back to my mind but I can't let that mess me up anymore, that was in my past and the Lord is helpin' me to forget all of that." She answered after a moment. "And I know that you and David think that this is some kind of phase or whatever but I know what happened to me in the hospital that day." She said as she remembered her conversation with Jane on Sunday.

"Do you remember what happened?" Michael asked her.

"I remember some stuff goin' on that seemed a little strange but I don't see what that has to do with all of these changes that both of you are goin' through." "It seems kind of cultish or somethin' and it's a little scary, no kiddin.'"

"If we were in a cult we'd be doin' some off the wall stuff but everything you've seen or heard us talk about is in the bible somewhere." Michael told her as he opened a bottle of hot sauce from the condiment tray.

"So the same thing that I saw happen to her happened to you too huh?" She asked him with a slight air of skepticism.

"April nineteenth." He said. "I wasn't in the hospital of course but Irene's mother had a lot to do with helpin' me to understand how much help I needed." He said, pausing.

"She's his best friend." Terry remarked.

"And you know it because if it wasn't for the way she broke stuff down to me, I know that I would probably still be tryin' to make it without God in all of the craziness goin' on out there." Michael said, shaking his head.

"So it wasn't Douglas that had anything to do with it huh?"

"He did but he probably didn't have any idea what he was doin'." "I got into trouble up there and to this day I haven't heard one word about it and that let me know that he's got somethin' that's more than a lot of talk." He answered. "I would hear all of these stories about what he was like when he was Junkyard and how one thing lead to another etc.etc."

"I could tell you some stories too but we won't go there, that was a long time ago." Doris said.

"It was but when I started to hear about how the Holy Ghost changed all of that for him then it started to make sense."

"And then when I saw what it did for him, it worked the same way." Terry said, referring to Michael. "It took more for me but whatever works." She added as she spread butter on a biscuit. "I mean it took me almost gettin' killed to get the message but I wouldn't go back for a million dollars after what God did for me."

"So did you ever find out who was involved in all of that?" Doris asked her.

"You might not believe this but one of those guys came back and asked me to forgive him and I didn't have any choice, you know what I mean?"

"Teresa Lynn Johnson." Doris said in shock. "You have got to be kiddin' me." She added as she raised her voice in indignation and disbelief at what she had just said.

"You heard me and you really don't have to yell Doris, it's all good." Terry calmly told her, unmoved by her reaction. "And I knew you would do what you just did once you found all of this out but this is one of those things that had to be done."

"And you probably didn't press one charge and send his tail to jail did you?"

"If I hadn't been the stupid one that started the whole thing I might've been able to do all of that but it wasn't worth it to me Doris." By that time I had started my life over again and what was I supposed to do, say yeah I forgive you but I'll see you in court dude, you almost killed me."

"What about the other four guys that he got to come in that room with him, where are they?" She threw at her.

"Doris you need to calm it down ma'am." Michael told her.

"Michael I can't help it, this is makin' me wonder if you've lost it somewhere Terry."

"I lost that nasty filthy lifestyle that I had and I'm not sorry that I didn't do it that way because that's not how the Lord wanted me to handle it, end of story." She said with quiet boldness.

"Okay, I'm sorry for yellin' honey but I can't understand how you can just let them get by with what they did to you." Doris said then.

"I can do that because of how God wiped my stuff out and it's not any of my business anymore what happens to them." She answered her.

"In other words their day is comin'." Michael remarked.

"But don't you think it would make you feel better to actually see some kind of pay back for what you went through?" Doris persisted.

"Even if I did, how would that change anything?" "I don't have time for that kind of stuff any more because I'm about tellin' people about how God got me out of my mess." Terry said with conviction.

"So you can just walk away from all of that like it never went on huh?"

"I have to, like I said, I don't have time to go there anymore."

"Do you mind if I tell David about well you're doin'?" Doris asked her. "He's been askin' about you."

"I'm gonna leave that up to you but I'll call him before we go back, if he finds out that we were here and I didn't try to call him, he'll make a big deal out of it."

"You didn't tell her about the rest of it." Michael commented.

"There's more?"

"Yeah, thanks for remindin' me." She told Michael. "Do you remember seein' all of that stuff on my hospital chart when you were there?"

"I couldn't believe my eyes when I saw all of the issues goin' on with you." Doris said. "They didn't find anything else did they?" She asked cautiously.

"When I went back for my follow up appointment, they couldn't find anything wrong, they ran my tests through twice because everything came back negative, they didn't wanna believe it."

"That's not possible." Doris said, shaking her head in doubt.

"It is when God gets involved and I know you don't wanna really believe that but it is what it is, there's no other explanation for it." Michael remarked.

"It's not that I don't believe in miracles and all of that but I've never seen anything like that happen to somebody that I know, it's usually somebody that you hear or read about it, you know what I mean?" She asked with a look of confusion on her face.

"Well you can't say that anymore, you're lookin' right at one." Michael told her as he reached for another chicken leg.

"Stand over there so I can get your picture together Michael." She suddenly said as she reached for her phone on the counter top behind them.

"Are you sendin' this to anybody?" He asked her.

"Not if you don't want me to but I am gonna print this off and frame it." She said as Michael stood right behind Terry before they both posed for her.

"I can't believe how good both of you look." Doris said a moment later as she wiped tears after looking at the photo on her phone. "How in the world?"

"Nobody but God, that's about all I can say." Terry said as she started to be moved by her reaction.

She nodded a little before speaking again. "And I'm sorry for the way I acted a few minutes ago but that just tripped me out honey, people just don't do that kind of stuff."

"But it was somethin' that I had to do and I know that it sounds crazy and I understand why that blew your mind because I would've done the same thing just a few months ago." Terry responded. "So don't feel bad about that, I didn't take it personally..."

"This brings it all home huh?" Michael asked two hours later as he and Terry drove around in her former "territory".

"You just don't know how much Michael and when I look around here, I'm thinkin', how did I let myself live like that?" She said as she began to be moved by the images of her past.

"We did things because we couldn't help ourselves and I don't know about you, but every time I see somethin' or somebody that reminds me of stuff that I was involved in, it just makes me so thankful." Michael remarked. "And I'm not any better than anybody else but I don't think I could go back even if if I tried."

"Why would you?" "It's crazy out there and I see that now and that's why I feel like I have to talk to anybody that'll listen to me." Terry said as she continued to reflect on the days that she had walked the street that they were slowly driving down.

"And everybody's not, I learned that from Douglas but the ones that do, it's worth it." Michael said. "And I really wanted to tell Doris about Andre' but I don't think it would've made that much difference to her."

"Right when we were leavin', she told me to pray for her and I could tell she meant it." Terry said as she suddenly noticed one of her old "co-workers" slowly walking towards the car. "Slow down a minute Michael." She told him after a moment.

"Do you know her?"

"I used to talk to her sometimes." She quietly said as she approached them after recognizing her.

"Where have you been?" She asked while looking over at Michael.

"This is my brother, I'm just down here for the day, I don't live here anymore." She said after he stopped and parked.

"Where'd you go, I heard you got busted." She said laughing at her.

She nodded a little as she got out of the car. "After that happened my brothers came down here and talked me into movin' up to Des Moines and I know that sounds crazy but it worked out, I'm done with this."

"So what did you do, find a really good job up there or somethin'?"

"I found a better payin' job but that's not why I gave this up." She said after a moment. "I almost got killed one night messin' around with people I didn't know and that knocked some sense into my head."

"Got you a new life huh?" She asked, giving her a high five.

"I did and I'm lovin' it."

"I'm glad for you baby but I got two kids to raise so I do what I gotta do." She said with a hoarse laugh. "So what are you doin' for fun, you used to tell me there was nothin' better."

"Don't remind me, I was stupid, and that was before I found out that God had somethin' better that I can't even really describe." She said as she felt her help beginning to rise up in her.

"Put this number in your phone and call me, I'm workin." She said as she handed her a piece of paper. "I gotta go, love you." She added as she spotted a car starting to slow down.

"Had enough?" Michael asked her a minute later as they watched her get into the car before they drove off.

"She nodded as she wiped her face with a tissue. "Let's go home.""...

CHAPTER 3

JUNE 18, THURSDAY

"I really can't explain it, they told me that things would be getting worse and ever since Sunday, I've only had to cough a couple of times." Florence remarked Thursday afternoon as she and Jane sat in the waiting area at the hospital before her two thirty appointment.

"And I want you to think about what you just said mom." Jane told her. "I think you know exactly why you're feelin' better."

"I went home and laid awake for two or three hours just thinking about how I felt after they prayed for me, and I had no idea that it was possible to feel God like that."

"It is, believe me." Jane told her. "And now you know for yourself so don't ever forget that because there's so much more for you if you believe it." She said as they were called back.

"We need to get another x-ray of your lungs to see if there's been any more changes in the tumors that we found last week." Florence's doctor remarked five minutes later in her exam room. "I've had a few consultations with some of my colleagues and we're all in agreement that we need to start your chemo treatment as soon as possible in order to stay ahead of this." He continued "We need to be as aggressive as possible so that we can have a positive outcome so a nurse will be ready for you in a few minutes to take you over to X-ray."

"Do you need me to go over there with you or do you want me to wait out there 'til they're done?" Jane asked her as she began to change into an exam gown.

"I'll be okay, just be here when I get back." She said nervously. "I'll be okay."

"Do you have any idea what's takin' 'em so long to get back in here?" Jane asked her an hour later as they contnued to wait for her doctor to come back in the room.

"When they got done with my X-rays, they said it would be a few minutes while the doctor looked everything over but I didn't think it would be this long." She said as they heard a knock at the door before her doctor came in with his colleague.

"Mrs. Steaven this is Dr. Kapp, I called him in for a consultation after I looked at your films this afternoon." He began as he sat down on a nearby stool. "And we don't use the word miracle loosely around here but we can't explain this any other way." He remarked as the second doctor put the before and after X-rays side by side up to the lighted viewer for them to see.

"This is what we found out last week and this is today." Dr. Kapp remarked as he compared the stunning contrast of the three malignant tumors on the left film, to the healed, cancer free lungs on the right. "And what we would like to know from you is what exactly happened between six days ago and today." "This is incredible."

"When she told me about it, we got together with a couple of other people that had enough faith to ask the Lord to take care of this." Jane remarked as she put her arm around Florence who was now crying out of relief and astonishment. "And that's exactly what happened." Jane added as she lost her own composure.

"We have seen faith do a lot of other things for people but this is the most dramatic that we have ever seen." "Your lungs look like they could belong to a twenty year old and that's not an exaggeration folks." Her doctor commented as they continued to examine the X-rays for any trace of what they had seen before. "It's incredible." He repeated.

"Is there any way that I can get a picture of these?" Jane asked him a moment later as she took her phone from her purse.

"If the patient is okay with it, I don't see why not." He said as Florence nodded through her tears, still unable to speak. "And with your permission, we would like to possibly write this case up in the A.M.A. journal because this is extraordinary."...

"When I called, Irene didn't tell me that you were on vacation this week." Jane told Douglas an hour later as she and Florence walked into the screened porch.

"So you found me huh?" He asked as he stood up to hug them both before they sat back down. "What's the good word?"

Neither said anything as Jane handed him the pictures that she had printed from her phone, while Florence sat there staring at him, still in awe at what had happened to her.

"This is what happens when you believe God." He barely spoke a few moments later after studying the pictures side by side.

"They're callin' it incredible and extraordinary." Jane remarked as he sat there taking in the work of the Lord that had honored their faith in Him.

"That pretty much says it all." He said as he continued to examine the X-ray images. "So how does this make you feel sweetheart?" He asked Florence as he wiped his face with a handkerchief.

"I feel like I owe you something-

He shook his head. "We need to talk ma'am." He told her as Jane got up to go in the house with Irene. "You don't owe me a thing, this is the work of God."

"Did I say something wrong?" She asked him a moment later.

"I said that because the last thing I want you to do is to feel obligated to me in any way." He began. "I didn't do anything except what the Lord led me to do and it was the power of God that healed you."

She nodded a little, trying not to feel intimidated by him.

"And number two, regardless of what you might think, I'm harmless and I cared about what was goin' on with you." He continued with a spirit of authentic love that she was beginning to sense in him.

"But you don't really know me Mr. Johnson, how could you put yourself in the place that you did?"

"I didn't have to know you and when Jane told me what was goin' on with you, that's all that mattered." He immediately answered her.

"And you did that even though we're different?"

"What does that have to do with it hon?" He asked her with gentle persistence. "I would've been totally wrong if I had let that stop us from doin' what we were obligated to do." "And I know how you think about all of that racial stuff, so let's just clear the air because I think that's botherin' you isn't it?"

She didn't answer but suddenly lost eye contact with him.

"You don't have to talk about that if it makes you uncomfortable and that's beside the point right now anyway." He told her. "But what happened to you is an outright miracle and if you let God help you, He has so much more for you."

"But why was I the one, I haven't been that good of a person." She said as she began to open up to him. "I have had friends and other relatives that have died from things that weren't as bad so I don't understand why I'm getting another chance."

"Another chance for what?" He asked in an attempt to keep her talking to him.

"Maybe I need to change the way I've been thinking for so many years and this could be God's way of doing that." She managed to say as she struggled to find the right words to express her feelings.

"That could be and if you feel like that's what happenin', then don't fight against it." He told her. "Nobody can do that except you and with the help of God, you can change if you really want to."

"Has Jane ever talked to you about the things that I might've said or done since she married Paul?" She asked as she allowed herself to "go there" with him.

"She has, and because I've known her and James for a long time, I've seen some of the things that they've had to put up with." Douglas said after a moment. "But because they have the Holy Ghost, they're able to deal with that kind of stuff in a different way than a lot of people would."

"I didn't know that you knew James."

"Yes ma'am, his wife and my wife are sisters so we're all connected." "Did Jane get a chance to show you who Chris is on Sunday when we were at their house?"

She shook her head in bewilderment. "I didn't have any idea it was like that."

"It is and James told me all about the day that he told you about her and I'm sayin' that because we need to get everything out in the open if you feel like the Lord is givin' you another chance with all of this."

"I understand."

"Nobody in this family is judgin' you and in fact, because of what you did for Paul and Jane and for what they decided to do for James and Chris, they're really thankful to you for how it all worked out." He told her. "They know that it all came from God in the first place but He put it on your heart to do what you did and they're blessed because of it."

"I did that because I could see that they needed more room but I didn't have any idea that it would work out like it did."

"Paul figured that it would make sense because it was more than he wanted to take care of by himself so James and Chris took him up on it." Douglas said. "And I have a question for you and it's up to you if you even answer it but I think it's doin' you some good for us to get things all out in the open." He said again. "The Lord helps us all when we start to see how much help we actually need and because of the way He just showed you such an awesome miracle, this is just the beginnin' for you."

She nodded again before reluctantly speaking again. "What did you want to ask me?"

"Do you think you would've given James the money that you did if you had known about Chris?"

At that, she admittedly shook her head as tears began to form in her eyes.

"How do you feel about that?" He patiently asked her as he continued to be led by his spiritual experience with souls.

"I feel awful about it and that's the reason I don't understand why something this great has happened to me."

"It's called grace and there's not a one of us that haven't experienced it." "When we wake up every mornin', that's called grace because none of us deserve the goodness of God but when He does things like this that we don't see everyday, it's life changing." He added while looking at the images again when Jane and Irene came out.

"Mom this is Paul's sister." Jane said a moment later as she introduced them.

"You look like him, I'm glad to meet you." She said as she started to extend her hand to her.

"Honey it's okay, we don't bite." Irene told her as she sat down in the chair next to her after noticing her apparent discomfort.

"I'm sorry, I apologize." She said with a nervous laugh.

"Jane just told me about your awesome news, how do you feel about that?" Irene asked her in an attempt to make her feel at ease.

"It's just a little hard to believe that something so wonderful has happened to me." She remarked after a moment after Jane and Douglas went back into the house.

"Don't be afraid to believe it, the Lord just showed you what He'll do with your faith so this is the time to be really happy and thankful for what just happened to you."

"I am but I was just thinking about what your husband was saying to me and I'm starting to feel pretty ashamed of myself about some things."

"You don't mind me askin' you what it was do you?" Irene asked her. "I might be able to help you out a little because until you get to know him, he can be a little scary, but believe me, when he cares about you and what happens with you, it's all about the truth."

She nodded a little in agreement. "And it wouldn't have come up if I hadn't told him that I felt like God was giving me a chance to change some things that I've done wrong in the past." She managed to get out.

"You mean with Paul and Jane and all of that black and white stuff?" Irene asked her with no reservations.

"How did you know that?"

"Because we've talked about that a lot since they got married but it hasn't always been that way." Irene began as she noticed her interest peak. "And I'm gonna tell you this because it was so long ago and it doesn't matter anymore but there was a time when I couldn't stand the sight of her." She admitted with regret.

"She never told me about anything like that."

"I'm sure she didn't but I'm just lettin' you know that that kind of stuff is on both sides and the only way that I was able to get rid of all of the hatred I had was because God gave me the Holy Ghost." Irene remarked. "Once I saw how off and wrong I was, that's when I got my help and I'm not sayin' that's the way you are, but that was me and my problem and I know what He can do if you let Him help you."

"He already did didn't He?"

"You'd better believe it, you have a testimony that not very many people do and we're here to help you in whatever way we can if you feel comfortable enough with us." She told her.

"And that was your mother that prayed with us on Sunday night?" She asked.

"It was, Douglas told me about all of that and I know she's really gonna have a good time with this news."

"I saw him when he became a little emotional about it too and I wasn't expecting to see that."

"If you don't know him, it is surprising because you don't expect somebody that looks like him to be that way." He can be really sensitive and he doesn't care who sees him cry over somethin' like that."

"I was married to Jane's father for over forty five years before he passed away, and I never saw him cry about anything so it's really different for me to see a man react like that." She said as she self consciously wiped her own tears.

"And he used to be totally opposite from what you just saw." Irene began as she handed her a tissue from the box on the small patio table between them. "Before we were married, he had the nickname Junkyard dog because he had this reputation of bein' mean and hard but God changed all of that."

"But he's such a kind caring man, how can that be?"

"It's all about what God can do if you want His help." "And He's already shown you just how powerful He is with the way you just got delivered from that sickness that you don't have anymore." Irene said. "And I don't know why I'm sayin' all of this to you but we just want you to know how blessed you are."

"Bascally it came up when she said she felt like the Lord was givin' her a chance to change some things." Douglas remarked with Jane up at the kitchen table. "And that's when she asked me if you had ever talked to me about some of the things that she might've said or done since you and Paul got married."

"So that's finally startin' to bother her huh?"

"She was the one that went there, I didn't bring that up but I could tell that was the source of the problem." Douglas remarked. "And since she brought it up, I told her that we need to get everything out in the open because that's how you get your help."

"How did that go?" Jane asked cautiously.

"It wasn't exactly a pretty picture but again, you have to get to the root of things if you're really serious about wantin' things to be different." He said after a moment. "So when it got to that point, I asked her if she would have given James that twenty five grand if she had known that he was married to Paul's sister."

"Oh ouch Douglas, you're a good one." Jane said, slightly amused.

"You have to fight fire with fire and I can pretty much guarantee you that she feels better since she came out and admitted that she wouldn't have."

"And you know what, that doesn't surprise me a bit."

"It didn't surprise me either because James told me how she reacted when he told her, but that's where we have to prove to her how much she's loved anyway, you know what I'm sayin'?"

"I do and I hope that this whole thing makes some kind of difference to her because I've been really wonderin' if all of the prayer and doin' the right thing has had any kind of impact on her after almost twenty five years."

"That's one of those things that only God knows but you can't ever give up on a soul, no matter what it looks like." Douglas told her. "If the Lord is leadin' you to keep prayin' and doin' whatever you have to do, there's no stoppin' until God does what He does and He does all things well."

"I know good and well that you're right but do you see how frustratin' it can be when you don't see any change in that long of a time?"

"I see what you're sayin' but it's not about what we see or don't see because only God knows the hearts of people." "And what you and Paul can do now is almost go out of your way to love her to the next level because you're all she has." "You can talk a big game 'til you're blue in the face but this thing that just happened to her is just the beginning because she's actually seen what the power of God can do."

"When we were on our way over here, all she could say was she couldn't believe it, over and over again." "Then when I tried to explain to her that this is what can happen when you put your trust in God, it was almost like she couldn't understand what I was talkin' about."

"And it might take a while before she really gets it, you know what I mean?" "When you're not used to seein' the things that the Lord can do, all you have in your mind is the natural to refer to." "This was a supernatural thing and to her, this is somethin' that might seem strange or impossible but to our mother-in-law Ms. Frances Michaels, she'll be happy about it but I don't think she'll be that surprised."

"Because she's seen so much before this."

"Exactly, now you're gettin' it." "And like that scripture in first Corinthians says, some things have to be spiritually discerned and when the Lord gets done with her, you're not gonna recognize her, mark my words, you heard it here first." Douglas said with confidence.

"You're probably right and that makes me think about Terry." "I was talkin' to her Sunday when she came over to see the house and I know what you and Michael went through had to be some hard stuff but she seems to be really gettin' it."

"When we see her now, it's like lookin' at a live walkin' miracle and she's proof that there's nothin' too hard for God, no matter how it looks."

"Didn't we tell you that God was gonna do the work honey?" Frances remarked an hour later after Jane and Florence sat down on the sofa across from her in the family room.

"I think she's still tryin' to process all of this, it's been pretty intense since we left the hospital." Jane answered.

"Well you know what my cure all is, why don't you go in there and fix her a cup of hot tea, I think Chris is in there fryin' chicken." She told Jane. "She'll show you where everything is."

"Will you drink it if I fix it mom?" Jane asked her. "If you don't feel like you want it, I don't want anything to go to waste."

She nodded. "I think that would be good." She answered as she struggled within herself to feel at ease with her.

Honey what are you nervous about, you're family in here." Frances told her as she got up to sit next to her. "We share nineteen grandchildren and the sooner we get on the same page with that, the better off things will be." She added as she put her arm around her.

"It's like Jane just said, I'm still trying to process everything that's happened today and it's a little overwhelming." She admitted. "We went to your daughter's house when we left the hospital and I got to talk to her husband again."

"And I know he was beside himself too wasn't he?"

"Jane showed him these pictures of my X-rays and he was really emotional about it." She said as she went into her purse and showed them to her.

"Did you know that I've been waitin' on this news?" Frances asked her. "And when he saw these, it meant a lot to him because when you see the work of God like this, it's such a blessing to know that He heard our prayers and did exactly what we asked Him to do." She said as she began to feel the Lord get in the conversation. "Jane said when she told him what was goin' on with you, he didn't flinch because we're not supposed to be intimidated by things like this." "It's a light thing for the name of Jesus to take care of whatever we bring to Him and He did it because our faith and confidence is in His name that is above every other name." She said with enthusiasm.

She nodded as her understanding to began to come open by her anointed words of truth, coming from a vessel that had witnessed the power of God in countless situations.

"And just to let you know how much the Lord cares about you and that situation you had, He wouldn't allow me to sleep Sunday night until I got down on my knees and started to thank Him for what He was about to do." She added. "And this is the evidence right here."

"But how did you know this would happen?"

"That's what faith is, it wouldn't have done us any good to ask the Lord for your healing if we didn't believe that He was gonna do it." She answered her without hesitation. "Have you ever had the chance to read in the scriptures about all of the people that Jesus healed when He was here?"

"I probably have but I never dreamed that I would see a miracle like this."

"Well we have and the same God that healed blind and deaf people and gave Sarah a baby when she was ninety years old is the same one that did this for you." Frances told her with confidence. "He brought dead people back to life and if we don't believe He's able to do things like this, then we have a problem."

"Is this the first time that you have seen a miracle like this?" Florence asked as her emotions began to overtake her.

"This is one of the greatest that I have ever seen but when Paul and his sisters were kids, I saw things that I'll never forget because I didn't any choice but to trust God." "I didn't have money to take them to the doctor, didn't have a car etc. etc. but I had the name of Jesus that took care of anything and everything and sometimes He'll allow you to be in circumstances so that He can prove Himself."

"Do you think that's what happened to me?"

"It could very well be and when you have a testimony like you do now, you shouldn't have any doubt in your mind about what He can do." "And this is a wonderful thing but He also promised you the gift of His spirit and that's even better because that's what will save your soul." "These bodies that we're livin' in are gonna die if the Lord

63

doesn't come first, but your soul is what He came to save." Frances said as Jane came back in with Chris then.

"Mom this is Chris, James' wife." Jane said as she introduced them.

"I heard about your good news, how do you feel?" She asked her.

"Without saying a word, Florence stood up then and reached out to her for a hug.

"I am so sorry." Was all she could manage to say as Chris returned her gesture.

"What are you sorry for, I'm not gettin' it." Chris said before suddenly remembering the incident between she and James.

"I am so sorry." She whispered again in her ear.

"Why don't we just act like none of that went on." Chris said as she sat back down a moment later. "We can talk about that later if you want to but I need to hear about your news." She added as she wiped her face.

"Since I've been talkin' to so many different people around here, I'm starting to understand some things that I didn't before." She began.

"So what did they say when they looked at these?" Chris asked after taking the pictures from Frances.

"They said that it was an extraordinary miracle and I'm still trying to figure out why God would do this for me."

"Honey we don't have to figure out everything that God does but the main thing is to give Him thanks and praise for doin' it." Frances told her.

"We have your tea ready in there if you still want it mom." Jane told her.

"And you might as well stay for dinner too, you look a little bit hungry." Chris told her. "Does that sound like a plan?"

"It does, let's go do it."…

JUNE 20, SATURDAY

"We were plannin' on stayin' 'til at least seven or eight o'clock but after we went down there where I used to work those streets, I couldn't stand it, I had to get back here Douglas." Terry remarked Saturday evening with him in his office. "Does that make me off or somethin'?"

"No honey that doesn't make you off, the Holy Ghost is changing your appetite from the things that you used to see and do, and there would be somethin' wrong if you still felt comfortable with that stuff." He told her.

She nodded then with understanding. "And while we were there on that block that I used to work, one of the girls that I knew saw us sittin' in the car." She said, shaking her head a little.

"Did she say anything to you?"

"She saw me and asked me where I've been and when I was comin' back." Terry said, thinking back to the conversation. "And I can't tell you how good it felt to be able to say that I wasn't."

"I know exactly how it felt because I've been there." He told her. "When I dropped out of sight and stopped runnin' the streets and wasn't showin' up in the bars and the clubs, I started to get phone calls from people that were wonderin' where I was." "This was back in the day before there was a such thing as a cell phone and I had a couple of 'em show up at home tryin' to find out what happened." "Then when I tried to explain that I was done with all of that, they thought it was a problem because I was the one that would keep stuff goin' out there."

"Really."

"If you ask Irene about those days, she could probably tell you about some things that I've tried to forget, but when you really have your mind made up that you're not goin' back to the things that the Lord saved you from, everybody isn't gonna understand that." "They're gonna be watchin' you and waitin' on you to slip up somewhere but you have what it takes to overcome all of that."

"And I think that's what Anthony is doin', he'll say and do things to get me to react like I used to and I guess I'm just gettin' the same stuff back that I would do with Michael." She said, laughing a little. "I was horrible."

"But whatever you do, don't feel like you have to apologize for the stand that you're takin' because you never know how your life is gonna affect somebody else's, whether you know it or not." Douglas told her from experience.

"I found out some of that when we went to see Doris."

"How did that go?"

"When we first got there, she couldn't believe that I wasn't still messed up from what happened to me, I think she was expectin' me to be like I was the last time she saw me."

"It's been over a month, how can that be?"

"I don't know but anyway, it was like she was tryin' to find things wrong, and then she asked me somethin' about what I ended up doin' to those guys that almost killed me."

"Did she try to make you feel bad for the way you handled it?"

"How did you know that?"

"I know a little about human nature and most people would call you crazy for the way you dealt with it."

"Andre' is the only one that I could actually i.d. and that was the main reason that I didn't do anything about it."

"Did you tell her about him?"

"I didn't because she wouldn't have understood what happened anyway and that would've given her more reason to come down on me about it." Terry said. "I mean that didn't bother me because I know I did the right thing even if it seems crazy but what else was I supposed to do?"

"You could've pressed charges and he might've been in jail by now if you had, but because you let the Lord lead you, he has the Holy Ghost now and it doesn't get any better than that." Douglas said as he began to search for a scripture for her to read.

"Is he doin' okay?"

"He is, I talk to him probably once a week and he's stayin' in touch with his grandmother which is really probably doin' her a lot of good."

"So how exactly did that go down?" Michael told me a couple of things but he told me that you could probably explain it better than he could."

"Michael had asked him to come by his house a couple of days after the Sunday you gave your testimony." He began. "He wanted to make sure that he knew that he was available to talk to and all of that good stuff."

"Michael said he didn't want him fallin' through the cracks." Terry said as she remembered their conversation.

"And that's a good thing." "When you come into holiness after livin' out there all of your life, you can shipwreck really quick if you're not taught what it's about." He said. "And that's why it's so important not to miss bible class and Sunday school and all of that to keep your spirit fed."

"I'm lovin' it, and I'm sorry that I didn't know anything about this before now because I could've saved myself from goin' through a lot of stuff."

"But you're young enough to be able to do a lot of good with what the Lord has given you so don't ever lose that." He admonished her. "And I'm tellin' Michael the same thing because you're still so new at this and it takes time to really get it but once you realize what a blessin' it is to have the Holy Ghost, nothin' will be able to make you go back."

"So that's why Michael wants to keep up with him huh?"

"That's it because the first thing the enemy will do is start puttin' things in your mind to discourage you and turn you back around." "And if you're not around people that can help you get through some things, it would be easy to find yourself right back out there."

"I think that's why Sheila calls me all of the time and that really does help when I might have a question about somethin' that I don't understand."

"And she's been around for a minute plus she's close to your age and that goes a long way." "When you have somebody around that's goin' through some of the same things that you are, it's easier to talk to your peers than it is to somebody my age."

"But we don't know what we'd do if we didn't have you to talk to Douglas, it doesn't make any difference that you're not our age." She told him.

"That's good to know but when you have a relationship with the Lord, that's who you go to first." "I might not always be around to talk to but there's one thing about God, He never sleeps and His ears are always open to your cry." He said, referring to Psalms 34:15. "And as far as people wantin' to criticize you about the way you handled the situation with Andre', you have this scripture to back you up." He said as he showed her Romans 12:19. "Read that and tell me what you get out of it."

"Dearly beloved, avenge not yourselves, but rather give place unto wrath: for it is written, Vengeance is mine; I will repay, saith the Lord." She read after a moment.

"Pretty plain isn't it?"

"Wow Douglas, I had no idea that this was in here." She said with surprise in her voice.

"And that tells me that you were led by the spirit of God and you can't go wrong by being sensitive to how the Holy Ghost is dealin' with you." He told her. "So what you did was free both of you up so everybody in the whole situation came out on top." "It started out pretty rough but you have to look at the big picture."

"Because if he hadn't gotten over like he did, he would've never known about Miss Barbara." Terry said after thinking a moment.

"That's exactly right and it was a matter of the Lord orderin' the steps of everybody involved from start to finish." "She hasn't really had anybody since Phillip died and that's been twenty years ago but because you were obedient, he got his help and it's been all good ever since."

"That is just a little unbelievable how things came together like that."

"When you use your natural mind, it is a little mind boggling but then when God decides to do somethin' like that, it just proves the amount of love that he has for every last one of us."

"Do you think that he might be able to talk to her about what happened to him?"

"The last time I talked to him he told me that he's gonna ask her to come to church with him so that's a start." Douglas said. "He doesn't have enough knowledge himself to do a lot of witnessin' but they can learn together if they make it a habit of goin' where they can get help."

"Have you seen her since that day she thought Michael was you?" Terry asked him.

"He told you about that huh?"

"Yeah he did and he thinks that she has some kind of obsession about you because you were with her son when he got killed."

"I wouldn't call it obsession but for some reason, she can't let go of that whole thing." He said after a moment. "And that's one of the reasons that I hesitate to call or go over there to see her because the conversation always ends up there."

"He was her only son wasn't he?"

"He was all she had until Andre' showed up but she makes herself feel worse because she's holdin' on to things that can't be changed." He said. "And I may not be the one to help her because I'm too close to it myself."

"Do you still think about that?" Terry asked him as she noticed the change in his voice.

"It'll try to come back every now and then, even after twenty years, but I can't let it distract me from what's goin' on right here and now." He answered her.

"But maybe there's still somethin' about it that you need to deal with Douglas." She said as she followed the leading of her spirit.

"I've wondered about that too because of the way things have happened." He admitted. "And I have enough God given sense to know when He's talkin' to me."

"You don't know what it is though?"

"I have an idea about what might be goin' on and this is one of those things that don't go anywhere until they're dealt with." He admitted.

"So how did you hook back up with her anyway?"

"Michael didn't tell you about that?"

"I remember him tellin' me about how you had to deliver Irene's sister's baby out in the middle of the street in the back of your van." Terry said, amused. "Wasn't that when she came out of her house to help you out with that?"

"I asked her if she had a bucket and some towels and it was almost like the whole thing was just meant to be." "From that day 'til the day we found out that Andre' was her grandson was beyond natural explanation and it was more than coincidence."

"And she asked you if you knew her son or somethin'?"

"She told me that I looked familiar to her but I don't remember ever meetin' her when I was runnin' around with Phillip."

"Maybe you just blocked all of that out Douglas." She told him.

"If I didn't take authority over those thoughts that try to come back to my mind I'd be right back where I started and that's not happenin'." He answered her. "And that's how you lose your victory, by dwellin' on things that used to be."

"But there's nothin' wrong with talkin' about what God did for you is it?"

"Of course it isn't, that's how people find out about how powerful He is but when you're always obsessin' over what you've been delivered from, sometimes it can sound like you miss that stuff out there."

"No way."

"You may feel like that but I've heard people actually brag about some of the stuff they were involved in and God doesn't get any glory and praise from that kind of talk." He told her. "And if I haven't told you this before now, I think you need to know that I'm proud of the way you've let the Lord use you since you've had the Holy Ghost."

"Really?" She asked him, again surprised by what he had just spoken to her.

"I am and I tell you that to encourage you to keep your faith up because it's not always easy to be obedient to what God wants from you."

"Why would it be that way?"

"For one thing, everybody isn't gonna agree with what you're doin' and you may find out how easy it is to get distracted by other things."

"But how do you get people to understand how much better it is to have this?" She asked with the innocence of a new babe in the Lord.

"Do you remember how you felt when we were talkin' about this to you when you first moved up here?"

"I thought Michael had lost his mind." She admitted after thinking a moment as she laughed at herself. "And it was different with you because I was too young to remember all of that stuff that David was tellin' me that you had done."

"It's the same thing and you don't understand it until it happens to you but the best way to witness to people is with your life." Douglas said, unmoved by her mention of David. "And believe it or not, people are watchin' to see if you're livin' up to what you say is right."

"Anthony said somethin' to me the other day that almost made me let him have it." She began. "But I'm really startin' to see how much of a difference it's makin' to have some power that's stoppin' me from doin' and sayin' things that are just wrong."

"He's testin' you and always remember that your mouth can get you in a lot of trouble so when you hear the Lord tellin' you to be quiet, you do just that and go on about your business." "You'll save yourself from havin' to go back and apologize for sayin' things that you didn't really mean."

"Have you ever had to do that because you talked too much or said the wrong thing to somebody?"

"I have and the experience taught me how to let the Lord take care of things that are too big for me to handle and it works every time." Douglas said after thinking a moment. "Before Irene got her help, she would try to provoke me into sayin' or doin' things that I had let go and it was one of those times that I almost let my flesh get the best of me." He recalled. "And I came close to tellin' her off but then it came to me that that wouldn't do anything but cancel out everything that she had seen up to that point and it wasn't worth it."

"But you told her that you were sorry anyway?"

"I did and she wasn't expectin' that because she had never heard me apologize to anybody about anything." "It wasn't in me to do that and even though she grew up around the church and she knew what her mother had been through and she had seen a lot of things happen, for some reason, she wasn't believin' that I could change like that."

"But like you said, you don't understand all of that until it happens to you." "And that's helpin' me to know why some people might look at me like I'm crazy when I try to explain what happened to me on May seventeenth."

"And whatever you do, don't ever take that day for granted because there are a lot of people that have left here without what you have." "It's the best thing that will ever happen to you because when it comes down to it, nothin' matters in the long run except Eternity."...

JUNE 21, SUNDAY

"I have never been to a church quite like yours and I really can't explain what it made me feel like." Florence remarked in the livingroom with Chris after dinner on Sunday.

"I've heard that before from people that aren't used to feelin' the presence of God when they go to church but that's what makes all of the difference." Chris told her. "And we want you to keep comin' back because we want you to see more of what God is doin' for people."

"I wasn't expecting it to be so integrated." She managed to say after trying to find the right words, cautious of offending her.

"You can say it, you don't have to walk on eggshells when it comes to that or anything else for that matter." Chris said as she detected her slight discomfort. "I mean James and me have heard and seen a lot of stuff over the last fifteen years so there's not too much that'll make any difference, you know what I mean?"

"Did you two meet at the church where we were today?"

She nodded."We went to the same school and church too so by the time we got married, we had known each other for years so it wasn't a big deal."

"But I think that it's really fascinating that you and Paul would marry outside of your race like you have." "It doesn't happen like that in one family very often but I've noticed that it's not an issue with anybody."

"Why should it be?" "God looks at the hearts of people and not what they look like and if we would start doin' that we'd be puttin' ourselves in a place that starts a lot of trouble."

"So you're saying that you and James have never had any problems because you decided to marry?"

"There's problems that come up because you're married but as far as the issue that you're talkin' about, it's just not there." Chris said. "The problem comes from other people that are on the outside lookin' in and would love to see us in trouble because of that."

"So what do you tell people?"

"For one thing, we don't give that kind of stuff any kind of audience because most of the time it doesn't do any good." "And I learned how not to get really attached to people after what happened with his mother."

You don't mind telling me what went on do you?"

"Not at all because it was so long ago that I've had time to get over it but at the time it happened, I was pregnant for the first time and I might've been more sensitive about things but it really did hurt." Chris said in retrospect. "We got married in June and six months later on Christmas eve, James' mother told him to come over by himself to the dinner that their family had every year." "It was just out of the blue and after all of that went down, his attitude about the way he was born totally changed."

"So that's the reason that he was so offended the day that I gave him the money?"

She nodded. "He told me you had said some things that really rubbed him the wrong way and that's why he reacted like he did." "He doesn't like to be identified with his race and of course that can't be changed so he deals with it as it comes." Chris explained.

"It's really unusual for people to feel that way about themselves isn't it?"

"It's a little different but I've heard of people havin' self hatred attitudes and he knows that he can't let that get the best of him because that's not what God wants." Chris told her. "And when you have the spirit of God, that makes all of the difference when you're keepin' it right with the Lord.

"But how long has he felt that way?"

"He told me one time he started to feel that way back when he was in grade school, maybe like fifth or sixth grade." She began. "One of his best friends was black and he started to get some flack about it from some of the white kids that noticed it and it's sort of built up for years."

"He doesn't mind that you're talking to me about this does he?"

"She shook her head. "I told him that I would probably be talkin' to you today and he'll probably be glad that I'm sayin' stuff that he doesn't really want to."

"Does he talk about it to anybody else besides you?"

"If he feels like he's really havin' a problem with it, Douglas would be the one that he would go to with it." Chris said. "When that thing with his mother went down he was the one that proved to be his best support and that's when they got to be as close as they are."

"He's quite a guy isn't he?"

"Him and my mother keep things together when stuff happens around here and I think that's why he was the first one Jane talked to after she found out about you." "He just seems to know what to do when things happen and after talkin' to either one of them, you just have a different perspective about whatever's goin' on."

"Do you mean things don't seem to be as serious after they talk to you?"

"That's a good way to put it and I think it's because they're intercessors, they spend a lot of time prayin' for people." And when things come up, the Lord has them do or say things that make a difference."

"When I got the chance to talk to him last week right after we found out about my good news, he said some things that really made me think about the way I've been since Jane married your brother." She began. "He told me that if I really wanted to change my mind about things that I need to get everything out in the open and that made me see my faults and how wrong I've been."

"And that's when the Lord can really help you turn some things around so that's a good thing." Chris said. "Everybody has somethin' to deal with but it's so much easier when you have the Holy Ghost to help you."

"That's what I heard about at your church today wasn't it?" Florence asked her then after thinking a moment.

"You remembered that huh?"

"I just can't get over how different your worship is and Jane has invited me before but I would always put her off." She said. "But since I've seen such a miracle in my life, that kind of changes things."

"Do you think you might come again?"

"I plan on it, I told Jane that I liked how free everybody seemed to be and I'm not used to that, but it was a liberating feeling there."

"Have you ever heard of that scripture that says that where the spirit of the Lord is, there is liberty?" Chris asked her.

"I don't think I have but it certainly seemed to be that way there." She said as she recalled her observation.

"Sometimes it scares people that have never been to a place where you can actually feel the presence of the Lord but that's when things happen." Chris remarked.

"That's the only place that you have ever gone to?"

"Yes ma'am, that's where my mother made sure we were so we wouldn't have any excuse about knowin' what the truth is."

"I was never like that with Jane and that's one of the reasons why her father and me were so surprised when she told us about what she was doing."

"I can remember James tellin' me about the mornin' that she received the Holy Ghost in their guest room when she came home with Lynn on Christmas break when they were in college." Chris said. "Did you ever meet her?"

"I met her once, does she still live here?"

"Her husband's job moved him to Cedar Rapids so they're not here anymore but she'll call to keep up with things goin' on here."

"So he was pretty young when that happened wasn't he?"

"He was ten years old but he remembers hearin' Jane speakin' in tongues late one night and he said that's when he started to understand what it meant to have the Holy Ghost."

"She has tried to talk about it with me but it never really made that much sense to me at first, but now that I know for myself how real it is all now, it's different."

"And you have a testimony that most people will never have because that doesn't happen very often." "When you hear cancer, most people think that's an automatic death sentence but it doesn't have to be that way."

"Has anybody in your family been healed like this before?"

She shook her head. "Nobody has ever had anything like that before we found out about my father a few months ago." "He had colon cancer but we didn't know anything about it 'til just before he died."

"When they were praying for me last week, they seemed so sure that it was going to happen and I just don't understand that kind of faith."

"When you've been through things, you know without thinkin' about it how much God will do for you when you believe Him and that's what it takes." "Have you told any of your friends about what happened to you?"

"I told my neighbor and I don't think she believed it but that doesn't stop me from telling other people."

"Everybody isn't gonna believe it but you can't let that stop you from talkin' about what you know is true." "And when the Lord sees that you're lettin' people know what He's done for you, He'll do even more."

"It's really encouraging for you to say that." She told her after a long moment. "And I know that this is a wonderful thing that has happened to me but there's still something that I feel is missing." She continued. "I mean I haven't wanted for anything for practically my whole life but after this experience, I feel like there's more coming."

"There is and I feel like the Lord wants me to let you know that He's gonna give you the Holy Ghost when you get to the place where you know that you need and want what He has for you." Chris told her. "He healed your body but your soul is what's even more important than that."

"Is that what's missing?" She asked as she reacted to her new revelation as if a literal light had come on in her spirit.

"That's exactly what it is." "Your soul is lettin' you know that it wants what the Lord said He would do when your heart is in the right place." "And it takes everybody different amounts of time to get to that place but if you talk to anybody that has the Holy Ghost, they have their own stories but the end result is the same."

"Michael and me were talkin' last week and I told him if we ask you and Aunt Frances the same thing, we'd probably get the exact answers." Janice remarked out on the deck at the table with Douglas, Terry, Sheila and 'Nita.

"Where is he anyway, how come he's not out here?" 'Nita asked.

"He's over there helpin' Paul do somethin', I made him a plate for later."

"So what's your question daughter?" He asked her after a moment in anticipation. "And have you already asked her what her answer is?"

"Not yet and there's nothin' deep about it but I just wanted to see how much you think alike." Janice said. "And my question is if you could go back in time what would you wanna relive in your life?"

"I think you already know and I'll tell you if you're right." He said without hesitation.

"The day the Lord gave you the Holy Ghost."

"Doesn't get any better than that on this side, I don't care what anybody says." He said as he reflected back. "You're talkin' to somebody that came out of some major wilderness and that day is the one I could do over and over again and not get tired of it."

"Major Groundhog Day huh?" 'Nita asked him.

"No comparison and when you think about what actually happened to you on that day, how can you not wanna go there again?"

"Tell me this Douglas." Sheila started.

"I'm listenin' ma'am."

"What is it that you're sayin' to people that always helps them get over?" She asked him. "I couldn't believe my eyes when you and Michael brought Andre' out of that room with the Holy Ghost after ten minutes."

"That's because he was ready, if you let the Lord lead you about people, you can pretty much discern repentance or if they're wastin' time." Douglas said as he thought back to the day. "No repentance, no Holy Ghost and I don't think we talk about that enough when we're witnessin' to people."

"And you're gonna change that, I already know." Sheila said as she poured more water in her glass.

"But it goes back to what I've noticed about some people that haven't heard this all of their lives." He began. "When you're fresh off the streets like he was, this seems to have more of an impact than it does to somebody that has heard about it year in and year out like your cousin Irene Michaels Johnson."

"Is that the way it was for you?" Janice asked him.

"You know it and after what I had been through, when I heard just what my soul was waitin' for, there wasn't any turnin' back." He said, thinking about his experience. "Then when you throw in some At the Cross and Glory To His Name, it was over." He said as he referred to the songs. "Junkyard was on his way out."

"So in other words, you're sayin' that the soul knows?"

"Now you're gettin' it." "If you don't get to the souls of people, you're not havin' any effect because everything else will come and go." "The drugs and the alcohol that people get caught up in can't satisfy the soul but when I came up out of that water after they called the name of Jesus over me, I lost a hundred pounds of sin in a second." He said as Terry suddenly got up from the table in tears as she recalled her own experience.

"I love it when she does that." Sheila said.

"And her story is one that still has me cryin' like a baby sometimes." Douglas said as Frances came out of the house with a plate.

"So Aunt Frances, you came out just in time." Sheila told her as she down next to Douglas.

"I just saw Terry in there lettin' the Lord bless her, what did I miss?"

"If you could go back in time, what would you wannna go back and live over again?" Janice asked her.

"Oh honey there's no question about it." She immediately answered. "And it's been over fifty years ago since the Lord gave me the Holy Ghost, but you don't forget the first time you feel that power and anointing in you, I don't care how long ago it was." "And if you have any sense, you don't let yourself ever get tired of that."

"I was right, I knew it." Janice said as she watched Sheila's reaction. "Wait 'til I tell Michael, he missed it."

"I love it, how does this happen?" Sheila asked.

"You have to remember that this is the person that wasn't afraid to tell me like it was back in the day when I thought nothin' would move me." Douglas said then. "And then when you get results from shuttin' your mouth and listenin', you start to think and talk alike."

"Obviously, it's almost scary." Sheila said as his ringtone sounded before he stood up after seeing Andre's name on the caller i.d.

"Somethin's up, did you see that?" Janice asked.

"What's up big mama?" 'Nita asked her.

"I don't know but somethin' is, watch and see."

"I really don't like to bother you on Sunday because I know that's when you're with your family and all of that but somethin' is goin' on with Miss Barbara that I've never seen before." Andre' told him a minute later as Douglas took his call in the family room.

"Are you with her now?"

"She went to church with me today and after we got back here, she started sayin' a lot of crazy soundin' things that didn't make a lot of sense."

"Can you remember any of it?"

"She started talkin' about you and my father again and how if it wasn't for you, he would still be here and all of that kind of stuff." He replied in a way that revealed stress in his voice.

"So what was your answer to that son?' He asked him in an effort to relax him.

"I wasn't tryin' to start anything with her but every time I go to see her, he comes up and I really wanna be able to help her with it, but nothing I say makes any difference to her."

"Then every time she wants to bring it up, try to take her in another direction altogether and if that doesn't work, sometimes you just have to walk away, you know what I mean?"

"I see what you mean but what I don't like is the way she wants to keep bringin' you into it." "It's like she's tryin' to turn me against you and you haven't done anything but help me."

"But I don't want you to feel like you have to defend me because I know how to handle her." Douglas said. "We've been through this over and over again and as long as she can find somebody that will listen to that, she won't ever stop."

"I mean I'm sorry that I never knew who he was but she wants to make it seem like you're responsible for what happened to him."

"Would it help if I talk to her again while you're there with her?" He asked after thinking a moment about the scenario.

"I had thought about that but I don't want to put you out any more." He said apologetically.

"Number one, you're not doin' anything out of order because you called me because this is what I told you to do when things come up." Douglas told him. "Do you have somethin' else that you need to do?"

"No sir."

"I can be there in fifteen or twenty minutes and this is one thing that I need for you to know." He began. "You're dealin' with one of two things and you did the right thing by lettin' me know what's goin' on and I'm gonna try to get Michael to come with me so sit tight, don't go anywhere."

"It's about time that you got here, what took you so long?" Barbara said half an hour after Andre' opened the door for Michael and Douglas.

"What's goin' on with you ma'am?" Douglas asked as he skipped any and all formalities with her.

"I talked to Phillip last night and he told me what really went on that night." She spued out with satanic venom that he immediately recognized as demonic forces speaking through her.

Then without saying a word, after noticing a pistol on the end table next to the urn with the ashes, he picked it up before emptying the cartridge of several bullets contained in it."

"What were you plannin' on doin' with this?" He calmly asked as he purposely made close eye contact with the spirit in her.

At that it began to repeatedly scream out vulgar obscenities directed at him in an attempt to distract from the inevitable and it was then that Douglas motioned Michael and Andre' over to stand next to him.

"Hold your peace and leave this vessel in the name of Jesus and you will not return." Douglas spoke with the authority of the Holy Ghost in a quiet but firm voice.

A moment later, Barbara screamed out as if in pain and fell backwards in the chair behind her.

"Oh my God, oh my God." Andre' said then in shock and amazement at what he had just witnessed.

"What I don't want to see you do is be afraid of what you just saw because you have the power to do exactly the same thing." Douglas told Andre' out on the porch a minute later after he sat down with he and Michael. "I wanted both of you to see the power that you have in the Holy Ghost that God gave you and He meant for us to be able to overcome anything that comes from hell."

"Is this the first time that you've seen somethin' like that?' Michael asked him, still trying to process what had just happened.

"It's not and we can't be intimidated by the mess that the devil tries and when you get the time, go through the scriptures when Jesus had to cast demons out of people." "He didn't hesitate to call it what it was and we have to be the same way, we have His spirit so what's the difference?" He asked them in an effort to stimulate their thoughts.

"None."

"And that wasn't actually her, it was a spirit behind all of that stuff that was comin' out of her mouth and it's up to us when we come across the devices of the devil to take care of business." He said with an air of finality and God given authority.

"I just thought things like that happened in the movies and I'm sittin' here trippin' out." Andre' said, shaking his head, still remembering the confrontation between the two supernatural forces.

"I can understand that because when you're not used to seein' the power of God work like that, it can be a little overwhelming." Douglas told him. "But this is your grandmother and you have the chance to love her to God so let your spirit lead you and you'll have the chance to do some things yourself." "Keep doin' what you're doin' and you'll see other things that you didn't think were possible and this is just the start of a new place that the Lord is leadin' you through so just get ready for it."…

Chapter 4

June 24, Wednesday

"Marie called last night and told me that mother's made up her mind to move here but she wants to make sure she has a place to go before she does anything else." Janice remarked Wednesday night with Frances in the family room. "She'll be here Friday night."

"So I take that to mean that she doesn't wanna move in with anybody else."

"She wants Marie to come and find a place for her to live before she comes herself so I guess I need to start lookin' around for some assisted livin' places."

"And she's on permanent disability because of the accident?"

She nodded. "She still has to go to rehab once a week because her hip was dislocated and she doesn't wanna have surgery for it." Janice said. Marie said she can't stand up for more than fifteen or twenty minutes at a time so she needs to live somewhere that doesn't have steps and all of that."

"I don't think that'll be hard to find but it's time to get started on it now because you don't have that much longer to go yourself." "You're not gonna feel too much like doin' stuff like that in a few weeks."

"That's why Marie's comin' so she can take care of that part of it." "She's gonna be here for a week and she's stayin' with Randy and Donna while we try to find a place."

"She left before Michael got here didn't she?" Frances asked as she sat folding laundry.

"He came right after they went back and he's sort of worried about her not trustin' him with me and the baby."

"That's because she doesn't know anything about him and it'll take some time for her to see that he's not messin' over you."

"I know it will but that doesn't keep her from startin' stuff with him."

"Honey don't let thoughts like that pull you down and take your peace of mind, you've come too far to let thoughts like that stress you out."

"I have but I know how she can be and when we talked a couple of weeks ago on the phone, she was tryin' to get me to back off so I wouldn't get hurt again."

"But that's not her problem, that's between you and Michael and if things don't work out, you'll handle it as it comes." Frances said. "Does she know that he's Douglas' brother?"

"I don't remember if I told her that or not but he's not one of her favorite people either so that doesn't mean that much to her."

"It doesn't have to but whatever you do, don't let yourself get into it about anything with her." "She's still your mother and even though things have turned out like they have, she has to be able to see the difference in you."

"Marie sort of told me the same thing and she warned me that she's always talkin' about how she wouldn't be in the shape that she's in if I hadn't left home in the first place." Janice said.

"She can't put that on you and if you really wanted to get petty about it, you could say if they hadn't reacted like they did when you told them that you were pregnant, you wouldn't have left and so and so on, you see what I'm sayin'?" "Don't let yourself get caught up in that kind of confusion because that's how the devil gets the upper hand sometimes." "You just can't go there with her."

"I'm gonna try not to." "Did you hear about what happened Sunday night when Douglas went over to Miss Barbara's house?"

84

"Irene told me what happened and the only reason she knew about it was because Michael told her."

"When he told me about it, he was still tryin' to figure out what happened."

"If you've never seen somethin' like that, it can be a little scary." Frances remarked. "But we have to be able to recognize the devil's stuff and that's all that was."

"He said he picked up that gun like it was nothin'."

"He hasn't forgotten how to do that stuff and it paid off didn't it?" Frances asked her laughing.

"He said there was six bullets in it and he gave 'em to Andre' and told him to get rid of 'em."

"And if he hadn't done what he had to do, it could've been ugly but when you stay on your knees, things like that don't intimidate you." "There would've been somethin' wrong if he had drawn back from that spirit and he knows that."

"But Michael said he won't really talk about it because he doesn't want anybody thinkin' that he's braggin' about it, you know what I mean?"

"And that's another reason why the Lord uses him like He does, he has an humble spirit and God hates pride." Frances said. "I can remember one night when your father tried to come at me with some crazy talk out of hell and all that is a device from Satan to scare you but we have the greater spirit and when you know that, you don't have any business givin' it the upper hand." "I looked right at that spirit behind him and talked to it just like I'm sittin' here talkin' to you."

"Was this before I was born?" She asked with hesitation.

"It was right before he left the first time and I don't know whether that was the reason that he took off but it never happened again."

"Is it gonna bother you to have her livin' here?" Janice asked after a moment.

"Because of what happened almost twenty years ago?" Frances asked her. "Honey I have moved on and he's in another place so what good would it do for me to hang on to that?"

"None." Janice admitted.

"And that's just another way for the enemy to throw you off from concentratin' on what really matters." "You were born for a reason and who am I to question the Lord for allowin' you to be here?"

"Sometimes I think that about the whole thing and I hope I don't make the same mistakes with Kristen that she made with me."

"You won't because you're trustin' God to show you what to do and not to do so don't get too far ahead of yourself."

"And if we decide to stay together, she's gonna know what's up from the start; she's not gonna grow up thinkin' one thing and then find out somethin' different later on."

"Is he givin' you any reason to think that you won't end up together?"

"He's not but we talked about it and we're gonna wait 'til she's born so he'll have a chance to get to see what it's gonna be like to take care of what's not his."

"She's not his by nature but if he'll be the one that'll be bringin' her up, then he's gonna feel like she is his."

"And that's somethin' else that we talk about a lot but until she gets here, he's not gonna know what that might be like." Janice said. "And it's because of that, I'm not lettin' myself really get into this like I should because he just might change his mind."

"Your heart is tellin' you one thing but then there's the practical stuff that's gettin' in the way." Frances said as she broke her thoughts down to her.

She nodded a little in agreement. "And he's bein' so patient with me."

"And if he didn't care anything about you, he wouldn't be hangin' tough with you like he is." "There's too many other girls around that he could get in no time but there was somethin' about you that he was attracted to, even before he had the right to be." "And didn't you tell me that you're lettin' the Lord lead you about each other?"

"Yes ma'am we are but there's just somethin' that's holdin' me back." She said as she let her emotions go.

"Then you keep doin' that and don't ever forget that big brother Douglas is watchin' him like a hawk, that's one thing that you can be sure of."

"I know but I don't want him to feel like he has to be that way, he has enough to deal with without havin' to do that."

"But that's somethin' that he takes more serious than you probably realize honey, don't ever think anything different." "If he thought Michael was takin' you for a ride, it wouldn't be a pretty picture. She continued. "And the way that the Lord had him step up to take your father's place should be enough to let you know that He knows how to take care of you." "Don't miss out on what the Lord has for you because you're feelin' a little insecure."

"I'm sorry, I need to stop it, you're right." She said after thinking a moment.

"I know I am and what you need to do is start livin' one day at a time and concentrate on this new life that you're about to have in a couple of months." Frances told her in a spirit of tough love. "Everything else will fall into place when you learn to stop leanin' on your own understandin' and be still and know that God is God and He's got it all under control."…

JUNE 26, FRIDAY

"We were talkin' Wednesday night after bible class and she told me some stuff that really made me feel guilty." Janice remarked with Douglas at the airport as they waited for Marie's flight around six-thirty.

"About what, did she take you to the woodshed?"

"We started out talkin' about mother movin' here and she ended up tellin' me to stop bein' so insecure about Michael."

"How did that happen, that's interesting." He said, glancing at his watch. "We have a few minutes, tell me about it."

"He came up when I told her that I wasn't gonna make the same mistakes with Kristen that she did with me." "If everything works out, she's gonna know everything so there won't be any surprises later on."

"So it sounds like you're not quite sure that it will."

"We've talked about it and we decided to wait until after she's born to give him some space and time to change his mind, you know what I mean?"

"And you're not willin' to allow yourself to commit because too many things can happen."

"After the other night, I'm gettin' there because Aunt Frances told me that if he wasn't for real, he wouldn't be hangin' tough like he is but my thing is, that's easy to do when there's not a baby yet." "I'm just tryin' to keep it real Douglas." She added.

"I can see that because nothin' about life is a hundred percent but you can't go through here bein' afraid to take chances either." "And for what it's worth to you, I'm prayin' about this right along with you and if I get somethin' from the Lord about you two, I don't have a problem lettin' you know about it, especially him."

"I didn't know that it mattered that much to you about what we do."

"It does because I don't wanna see you get into somethin' that you might regret later on after it's too late." He told her. "Both of you have the Holy Ghost but that doesn't mean that you won't have some problems and issues to deal with."

"I know, Chris tells me that a lot and when I watch her and James, they don't let things get out of control like I used to see when I was growin' up." "They would always be goin' at it about somethin' and that's all I knew 'til I came here and saw that it doesn't have to be that way."

"Of course it doesn't but it takes a lot of time and patience to get to that place because marriage is a lot of work." "That's why it's so important to make sure that you love each other because it's gonna be put to the test, believe me when I tell you." He added as she listened intently to his "words of wisdom."

"Is that why so many people break up?"

"Everybody has their own reasons but you can avoid a lot of issues just by talkin' your problems out and if you do it like the Lord set it up, you'll make it." He said. "But for right now, try not to get overwhelmed by more than one thing because that's how you get stressed out and that takes your peace of mind away." Douglas concluded as they noticed Marie coming towards them from the escalator, obviously glad to see them.

"Let me have my hugs." She said as she approached them.

"I know, I can't hide it anymore." Janice said as she took notice of her growing bump.

"Just hush, you're almost done." She said. "It looks like you're takin' good care of her." She told Douglas after they quickly embraced a moment later.

"We're helpin' each other." "How's Jerry?"

"We'll talk." She said as they approached the luggage carousel. "I tried to get him to come with me but he couldn't get off and like I said, we'll talk."

"I fixed up a room for you and I'm still unpackin' boxes so just overlook all of my stuff." Donna said an hour later as she and Marie started upstairs.

"It's just me, I'm family, don't worry about it." She said. "And it looks altogether different than it did when Chris and James were here."

"I'm tryin' to get it together but Sara's just six weeks old and I'm still sort of gettin' over that experience."

"Janice told me about that right after it happened but you don't even look like you just had a baby, you're doin' good."

"For one thing, I'm still gettin' used to these steps and it's not goin' too well." She said laughing a little as they started towards the guest room.

"They just don't build houses like this anymore, I love these huge bedrooms." Marie said as she put her bag down and sat down on the bed.

"But James made sure that their new house have the same room dimensions as this one because they need all the space they can get."

"Yeah I heard Chris is pregnant so they're gonna really have a houseful." Marie said. "But tell me this, how serious are Janice and Douglas' brother, what's his name Michael?"

"She told me the other day that they're waitin' til after she has the baby before they decide to do anything." "And that's smart, there's no rush, she's been through enough this year already, they need to take it slow."

"When am I gonna get to meet him?"

"Check with Janice, she knows his schedule better than anybody else; he works the third shift so it's a little different."

"She seems to really have it together, I told Douglas that he must be takin' good care of her."

"And you know it and after we found out that she was our sister because of what happened-

"Say that again?" Marie told her in total shock.

"Aunt Kathryn didn't tell you?" Donna asked her.

"Tell me what Donna?" She asked. "I can take it, whatever it is."

"Janice is our half sister and not our cousin like we thought."

"You mean you and Chris and Irene and Paul are her sisters and brother?"

"Half but we decided to drop that." Donna said.

"Oh my Lord, let me think about that for a second." Marie said as she processed what she had just heard.

"I just thought you knew Marie, she didn't tell you?"

She shook her head. "And I know that my Holy Ghost is workin' now because if you had told me this three months ago, I would've been cussin' and cryin' and all of the above." "Oh my Lord." She said again. "But you're gonna have to back up a second, how did this come out?" "And how is Aunt Frances?"

"She's been like a rock through this whole thing and we found it out when daddy came home sick back in April and he wanted to see Janice before he died."

"Well no wonder Janice could tell that he always made a difference between us, it's all clear now." She said shaking her head, thinking about Roy's behavior towards her. "He knew he wasn't her father and he probably felt like he didn't have to act like he was." She concluded. "But why didn't she tell me when everybody else found out?"

"That's somethin' that you're gonna have to ask her, I don't know why she would keep it from you."

"So this means that Janice and me are just half sisters too doesn't it?"

Donna nodded. "You have the same mother but different fathers."

"What did that do to her when she found out?"

"She took it pretty hard at first because it made her feel like she was just out there, you know what I mean?"

"And that's when Douglas really took over didn't he?"

"I really don't know what she would've done if he hadn't." Donna remarked. "I mean we know what the Lord does when stuff happens but He's used Douglas from the beginnin' to get her through some stuff."

"Yeah when I get the chance I'm gonna talk to him about that and some other stuff I'm dealin' with." Marie said, distracted for a moment. "But back to this other thing, what did Aunt Frances do when she found this out?"

"She called your mother to make sure that it was true, and after she admitted it, it was like this calm came over her like it just didn't matter anymore."

"How do you get to that place Donna?" "When I was here before, she was talkin' to me about some of the things that she's gone through and it was like no big deal."

"When you go through like she has, you get a thick skin and things like that don't really affect you because you know that God has your back." Donna said. "She even told us that we might have some more half brothers and sisters across the country that we'll never know about."

"She's probably right." Marie said in agreement. "But I don't know why mother didn't tell me after everybody else found out."

"That's not somethin' that you would just bring up out of nowhere and maybe she figured that Janice would eventually tell you."

"I need to talk to her too then and I guess I should get it over with, I don't want anything to get in the way of us findin' mother somewhere to stay."

"Just get it out in the open and make up your mind not to judge Aunt Kathryn, we don't know what went on except that Janice is here for a reason."

"That's a good way to look at it." Marie said after thinking a moment. "But I guess I need to put that on the shelf for a minute and concentrate on why I'm here huh?"

"Have you found any place that you think she'll go for?"

"Janice got on the internet and found a couple of places that might work for her so tomorrow mornin', we're gonna go check these places out and go from there." "We have to start somewhere."…

June 29, Monday

"When she introduced him to me at church yesterday I was thinkin' this must've been the way you looked twenty years ago; I was shocked." Marie remarked in the kitchen with Irene and Douglas after dinner Monday night.

"Everybody says that, we're used to it."

"And your sister doesn't look anything like you but you can tell you're in the same family by her mannerisms and the way she talks." Doris said as Irene set a cup of coffee in front of her. "Her and Sheila had somethin' goin' on but she said she wanted to get together before I go back to D.C."

"Can you see that comin' together?" Irene asked her.

"He seems to be really crazy about her and if they do work things out, she'll have a testimony that most people don't." Marie remarked. "And how exactly did that happen anyway, you don't see men go for somebody that's carryin' a baby that's not his."

"He saw her one time and he hasn't looked back." Irene said. "Mother says that's a God thing and she might be right."

"I didn't tell you that I'm just now findin' out that she's our half sister did I?"

"Are you serious?"

"Donna thought I knew and she just happened to mention it the other day and I'm still tryin' to process the whole thing." Marie said, shaking her head a little. "I haven't said anything to Janice about it because she seems to be pretty much over it and I don't need to start it up again."

"Sometimes she'll say things that let me know that she's still feelin' some issues behind all of that, but for her to be so young and dealin' with so much, she's on top of it for the most part." Douglas spoke up.

"And I know that you don't wanna take any credit for that but you probably don't know how much of an effect you've had on her." Marie said. "I mean it's amazing how much you see in retrospect because since Friday when I found this out from Donna, my mind has been goin' back to the last fourteen or fifteen years when we were growin' up." She said as she got a napkin from the holder.

"What was goin' on Marie?" Irene asked her as she sat back down.

"I was layin' awake Friday night and askin' the Lord to help me with this because now I'm startin' to remember stuff and the difference that he made between us." "He knew she wasn't his so he wasn't goin' out of his way to act like he was." She continued.

"Was it really obvious stuff?" Irene asked her as Douglas sat quietly taking mental notes.

"When I think about it now, he would spend more money on me than he would her and he would say things that weren't true to make her feel bad." She began after thinking a moment. "And I know good and well that mother had to notice stuff like that but I don't remember her ever sayin' anything about it to him and those little things were just the tip of the iceberg."

"She might've tried to talk to him but he might not have paid her any attention and that's one of those things we may not ever know." Douglas said.

"And I've thought about askin' her if she ever noticed the things that he would say and do but then it was like, it wouldn't really do any good to open that can of worms." Marie remarked.

"And you said she doesn't know that Donna told you?" Irene asked her.

She shook her head. "Not yet but before I leave, I plan to sit down and tell her how I found out and that it doesn't really change anything between us just because of what happened nineteen years ago."

"And she needs to know that and the more people she has supportin' her the better because this might not go away over night." Irene remarked.

"She might seem to be handlin' it okay and it might be different if she was twenty five or thirty years old findin' this out." Marie said. "But she just turned eighteen and that's a big difference; this is recent stuff and Douglas, you're actually the first positive relationship that she's had with the opposite sex." "And how sad is that?"

"How long did she know Craig?" Irene asked her, disturbed.

"She went to school with him and they had only been datin' or whatever you wanna call it for maybe two or three months before she got pregnant." "And we know how that went, she was just somebody that he used up and went on to the next one."

"Do you ever see him around?"

"I saw him at the mall one day with another girl that looked like she was about to pop and that just let me know how well off she is now to be away from that whole environment." Marie said. "And it's really somethin' how God has changed my mindset because when I was here back in April, I couldn't understand why in the world she did what she did by leavin' home but now I see a hundred percent why she did."

"Did Donna tell you how she reacted when she found out that Uncle Roy wasn't her father?" Irene asked.

"I didn't think to ask her that but I was gonna see what you had to say about it."

"We had thought about not tellin' her but that wouldn't have worked because he wasn't gonna be satisfied until he got his chance to see her before he died." Irene told her.

"So if he hadn't come home and dropped that bomb, we would've never known."

"Probably not so all of this was probably meant to be but we had James bring her over to mother's house and she sat her down and told her that we were her sisters instead of her cousins like we all thought."

"And it probably took her a minute to put two and two together didn't it?"

"It did and once mother broke it down to her, it was like her mind started to go back to all of the stuff that you were just tellin' us about and that's when it clicked." Irene said. "And mother said it was just like clockwork; it was almost scary the way you walked in there right when she pretty much lost it." She said to Douglas.

"Are you serious?' She asked him.

"I didn't say anything and neither did she but sometimes body language will talk better than your mouth can and it was like an unspoken thing that's a little hard to explain."

"And that was when mother told her that this was her father now so it's okay to do what you have to do and she didn't argue either." Irene concluded. "It was like she was five years old again so you can imagine how emotional that moment was." She said as Marie allowed herself to be in "that moment" she had just described by letting tears fall freely down her face as she got another napkin from the holder.

"So how does this make you feel Douglas?" She asked him after a moment. "And I don't want you to hold anything back either." She added as she gradually regained her composure.

"What it's doin' is makin' me more determined that my other girls don't go through what she's had to endure, you know what I'm sayin'?" He said without hesitation. "And it's a two way street; I can't really put into words what's it done for me because it's helpin' me to keep myself in check." "I don't take this lightly at all."

"Do you know how unusual it is for you to be willin' to step up for her like you have?" She asked him.

"It might be but it doesn't really matter who does or doesn't do because I have to go with the way the Lord has led me and believe me, I did a lot of prayin' about it before I put myself in this position." He said. "And nobody knew that this was comin' but when it did, it wasn't a problem to do what had to be done."

"And the Lord is gonna really bless you for this one day, watch and see." She said.

"So how has it been with Jerry the last couple of months since you came back home with the Holy Ghost?" Douglas asked as he directed the conversation from himself.

"Do you remember when we were talkin' about this right before I left back in April?" She asked both of them.

"We do and I've been prayin' a lot for you because I haven't forgotten about horrible I was, and how hard I was to live with." Irene answered her after a moment.

"It's been a lot different because he doesn't understand why I don't want anything to do with the way we used to do things, you know what I'm sayin'?"

"You know I do and it started from day one ma'am." Douglas told her.

"When he picked mother and me up at the airport, he took one look at me and said what happened to you?" She began. "And I had called him a few days before we got back and tried to tell him what was goin' on and he probably thought to himself, yeah right, whatever."

"But when he actually saw you it was probably altogether different." Irene said.

"It was because when he left me here, I had just been through that craziness that I tried to do to myself." She said, shaking her head as she remembered the night of her suicide attempt. "I think that he was expectin' to see me just like I was that night and it kind of blew his mind when he saw that I wasn't."

"But wouldn't you think that would be a good thing?" Irene asked her.

"You would think so but I'm findin' out that he would rather see me messed up like I was because that gives him an excuse to leave or keep stuff goin' with me."

"I can remember bein' that way and that's not anything but a device of the devil to discourage you from doin' what you know is the right thing." Irene told her. "I didn't like it because he was gettin' himself together and I didn't want anything to do with it." "Just a horrible spirit and I knew from that Sunday night when he came home from church that somethin' was different."

"So you didn't get it that first Sunday that you told me about?" Marie asked him.

"It took me a week from one Sunday to the next Sunday night for me to understand what was really goin' on." Douglas said. "I didn't have any idea what it meant to repent from anything, I was fresh off the streets." He recalled. "So they took me aside, broke it down to me and after what I felt when I came up out of that water, I wasn't gonna be satisfied 'til I had it all."

"When I called mother the Saturday night she talked to him on the phone and told him to come to church the next day, I thought you were gonna go and then maybe let somebody pray for you or somethin'." Irene said. "I knew how it worked, I had seen people go up to the altar and get prayer for years, week after week and I thought that would be the end of it." She said, starting to laugh.

"But the Lord had other plans huh?' Marie asked him.

"And you know it, I went up there to the front after they started singin' At the Cross and I was done, my soul knew and that was the beginnin' of the end for Junkyard." He added.

"Then when I saw them take him back there to get baptized, that's when I started to panic." Irene admitted. "I wasn't lettin' on but I had a problem with that."

"I didn't get it in the water like you did but I wasn't gonna stop 'til I had everything the Lord had for me, and after they explained to me what the Holy Ghost is, I was on a mission."

"And it took a week for that to happen huh?"

"It did but it was worth everything I went through to get it and that's why you have to be so patient with people." "You might be surprised at the number of people that have never even heard of what this is and if we're not careful we'll start to take it for granted and I refuse to let that happen."

"Has Jerry gone to church with you yet?" Irene asked her.

"A couple of times but his thing is not wantin' to let go of things that he thinks he can't live without." Marie said. "And one of the first things that we got into it about after I got back was his smokin' in the house." "I opened the door when we got back from the airport and almost got sick from the smell and it never used to affect me like that before." "I've never smoked and I would put up with it but I just can't anymore."

"Does he know how dangerous that second hand smoke is?" Irene asked her.

"I told him that and that's when he stopped but I can tell that he still has a problem with goin' outdoors every time he wants to light up." Marie said. "He keeps tellin' me that he wants to quit and one day I told him that the Lord can take that addiction away if he would let God help him."

"What was his answer to that?" Douglas asked her.

"He won't talk about it but I've just made up my mind to keep prayin' for him because if things keep up like they are, I might come home one day and he won't be there." She said shaking her head a little. "And I remember you tellin' me that you had gotten to that place and I could hardly believe it." She told Irene.

"Yes ma'am, I was about to file for a legal separation and I told mother what I was thinkin' and she went and told Paul on me." She said, laughing.

"You didn't tell me about that before when we were talkin' about this." Marie said. "So what did he tell you?"

"He basically got in my face and told me to get over it and I needed to be glad that I had somebody that loved me." She began.

"And then when he told me I needed to get it together and do the same thing that he did, that's when I finally started to get over myself."

"After knowin' what to do for years and that's what I don't quite understand baby, what took you so long?" Douglas asked her.

"I probably thought I was cute and I wanted to get out there and do my thing, I didn't have time for that." She answered. "That's why you met me in a club where I didn't have any business."

"Did Aunt Frances know that?" Marie asked, amused at her.

"I used to lie and tell her I was spendin' the night with a girlfriend I knew from high school." She admitted. "I thought I was grown just because I was eighteen and I would hang out at these places 'til they closed at one or two in the mornin.'"

"Did she ever find out what you were doin'?"

"I tried to sneak in one night around three o'clock and there she was, waitin' up for me and I got busted big time."

"I know she doesn't play that stuff and she's still that way." Marie said. "I noticed how Chris and James' kids don't give her any problems either and I guess you have to be that way because they have to know who the boss is."

"Have you ever talked to her about you and Jerry?" Douglas asked her.

"When I was here in April, I remember askin' her how she got through so much without goin' crazy but that was before I knew better." "I know now how she's still in one piece and it's even more amazing to me since I found out how Janice got here."

"She's livin' proof of 'til death do you part and I know what it's like to be in your situation." Douglas told her. "And if he's willin' to stay with you even though things are different, what choice do you have except let God work on him through the things you do or don't do."

"And I don't have a problem with that, my pastor at home told me the same thing." She remarked. "But we were havin' problems before and sometimes I think he's just waitin' for the right time to tell me that he's done." She said with a remorseful shrug.

"And you can't make him stay if he's already made up his mind about that but that doesn't mean that you can't get married again if it works out that way."

"He told me that too; he showed me that scripture in Corinthians, is that where it is?"

"That's the one, first Corinthians seventh chapter, verses ten through sixteen and I can't tell you how many times I had to go back and read that to keep myself encouraged and one day it paid off." Douglas told her. "Paul had a little to do with it but the end result is what matters."

"So I don't need to give up huh?"

"No way honey, the Lord can heal your marriage." Irene told her. "We know that through experience and sometimes the worse it looks is when you start to come out."

"That's what it's gonna take because it's too much for me to figure out." She said with resignation. "And I know that it'll take some work, just like you said, but if it's all on one person, I'm wastin' my time."

"Have you ever just come out and asked him what he's thinkin'?" Douglas asked her.

"I haven't yet because I'm afraid of what he might say, you know what I mean?" "And there's a side of me that's wonderin' what he's doin' while I'm here because I really wouldn't be that surprised if somethin' else was goin' on."

"Have you talked to him since you've been here?" Irene asked her.

"I called and left him a message to let him know that I got here ok." She said as she twisted her wedding ring around on her finger. "And I know now what it means to have peace when stuff is goin' on; a few months ago, I would've been stressin' out big time."

"That's how you get your victory because even if things don't work out the way you want 'em to, your peace of mind will kick in and you just move on." Douglas said. "When you think about what happened to you a couple of months ago, how can you not make it through this?"

"It'll be three months next week and when things try to mess my mind up, I start to think about that night and it puts everything in perspective." She said. "And he doesn't understand why I've stopped watchin' certain stuff on t.v. and I'm not goin' out with him on the week-ends and on and on it goes but I can't go back to what God got me out of."

"And he's not gonna understand any of that because it takes the spirit of God to change your mindset." Douglas said.

"I'm findin' that out and then he'll accuse me of bein' on some kind of self righteous trip and one thing leads to another but I'm learnin' how to keep my mouth shut." She said.

"That's the best way to keep things from gettin' out of control but at the same time, he's gonna have to understand that there's certain things that you won't be doin' anymore." Douglas remarked as they continued to patiently listen to her.

But you didn't have that problem did you?" She asked Irene.

"I knew what was up because I lived with mother all of my life." Irene said after thinking a moment. "And even though I didn't have the Holy Ghost, I knew when he came home that night that things just weren't gonna be the same and I didn't like it." She admitted.

"And she made sure I knew it too but after what I had been through, I was done with the world." "It was one of those things that I had to say in other words, honey you're just gonna have to get over it and I still love you but things are different now.

"And that's what kept me from actually leavin', seriously." Irene spoke up then. "I started to notice how he was talkin' to me in an altogether different way, there wasn't anymore cussin' and fussin' goin' on and it was those small things that started to work on me after a while." She concluded.

"After I started goin' to a few bible classes and found out that I was supposed to be lovin' her like Jesus loves the church, then that's when I had to start lettin' the Lord change me." Douglas said. "And you might be surprised how much power love has when you're in the kind of situation that you're in." "It works every time."

"Even when it feels like it's not doin' any good huh?" She asked him.

"Exactly and I'm not gonna sit here and say that it was an easy thing when you know that other person is workin' against you and

101

tryin' to provoke you into doin' things." "That's not anybody's joke but it can be done when you let the Lord keep you out of your flesh."

"Did I ever apologize to you for the way I acted for almost a whole year?" Irene asked him.

"Probably not but it doesn't matter now because you taught me how to do it God's way and that makes it all good."...

JULY 2, THURSDAY

"When Janice called and told me that you were comin' to take me out to lunch I got excited." Marie remarked Thursday afternoon after she and Michael had been seated in a restaurant booth.

"I couldn't let you come to town without spendin' some time with you because I don't know when you'll be back." He said as their menus were set in front of them by the hostess.

"I might be able to make it back when she has Kristen; I'm not sure about that but I'll deal with that in three months." She said. "And it's almost scary the way you and Douglas look and act almost exactly alike." She said as she "observed" him.

"I get that a lot, the only thing missin' is the beard huh?"

"Pretty much." She said, agreeing with him as she began to look through her menu.

"Janice told me that you found a place for your mother to stay." He said as he changed the subject from himself.

"We did and I hope she's okay with it because she told me that she trusted us."

"How far is it from James and Chris?"

"Not that far, we did the mileage after we got her on the waitin' list and its pretty close to five miles from their house." "It's called Edencrest Village and I sent her some pictures of it. "She said as she pulled up the website on her phone to show him.

"I think I've seen this place, how long will it take for her to get here?" He asked after looking at the advertisement.

"We're gonna try for the last of August, that's the soonest they'll have an opening."

"And she's due the last of September or the first of October so that gives her time to get settled in."

"You're on top of it aren't you?"

"Next to the day that the Lord gave me the Holy Ghost, I haven't been this serious about anything for a long time." He said after a moment. "And this is the main reason that I wanted to get together with you before you go back; I don't want you or your mother to have any worries about Janice and the baby if we decide to stay together."

"I can tell that you're crazy about each other just by what I've seen in the last week so I'm not really worried about that part of it." Marie said as the waitress approached the booth.

"So that means that you're concerned about what may happen after she has the baby." Michael continued two minutes later after they ordered." And I'm just keepin' it real, Douglas has taught me to get things out in the open, that's how you deal with issues."

"I had dinner with them on Monday night and I can't tell you how much they helped me out with some things." Marie said.

"That's because they've been through a lot together and you can believe that he's watchin' me like a hawk when it comes to Janice and me."

"I know he is, he said that he's not takin' that relationship lightly and I believe it." She said.

"And because he is, it's helpin' me to see what that's all about."

"Is he anything like your father is?"

"They're like night and day and that tells me that it has to be the Lord leadin' him because he wasn't exactly the father type, you know what I mean?" Michael asked her.

"In a way I do and I don't want you to feel like I'm puttin' you through some kind of third degree about Janice and this baby but I'm just a little curious about somethin.'" She asked him as she opened her straw.

"Let me have it, this is the time to do it." He conceded.

"Why didn't it make any difference to you that she was pregnant the first time you met her?" Marie asked him. "That just really surprises me because that by itself would run ninety-nine percent of men away."

"Then I guess I'm in that one per cent that overlooked that for some reason." He said as they laughed together. "But when I look back on that day, I probably had my nerve by assumin' that she wasn't with the baby's father because I was a man on a mission." He admitted, shaking his head. "I had just moved up here from St. Louis because I lost my job down there, and I was runnin' around with Douglas." He said, pausing as he thought back to the day. "We stopped at Chris and James' house, then when she walked in there with him from work, I saw this pretty girl with a baby bump and I was done."

"Wow Michael, that's crazy." Marie said, fascinated with his "story."

"It gets better." He continued. "Chris told me later that her and Douglas both had noticed how I was checkin' her out and that's when he took her aside one day and warned her that I was probably gonna make a move." He said.

"Just like a father."

"He's serious." "She had just received the Holy Ghost maybe two weeks before I showed up and he was leavin' it up to her to get me told." "He could've told me what was up but he figured that it would be more effective comin' from her and she didn't have a problem when the time came, believe me."

"I had no idea all of that went on." Marie said.

"It did and I was talkin' to Aunt Frances about this whole thing with her and she thinks that God has been in it from the start."

"She might be right."

"She usually is." "She gave me some homework and told me to read about Jacob and Rachel in Genesis and that guy was determined to get what he wanted." "He was on a mission too."

"With one difference."

"I knew you would go there, Rachel wasn't pregnant, but the only way to prove myself is to let time take care of that." "And I see where you're comin' from, I'm puttin' myself in you and your mother's place."

"So you understand that huh?"

"I do, you don't wanna see her go through another major mess in her life and I don't either."

"But I think the things that have happened have made her stronger because this time last year, she was a totally different person."

"She was still in high school wasn't she?"

"About to start her senior year; she went to summer school so she could could graduate in January." Marie said. "And that's when she found out about Kristen but I think she knows now that you have to live with the decisions you make."

"Do you think he took advantage of her?" He asked, referring to Craig.

"I've wondered about that myself and I know he probably didn't rape her or anything but he could probably tell how vulnerable she was." "It was probably easy for him to convince her that he cared about her and all of that stuff and she believed it."

"And knowin' that, there's no way that I could let myself do that to her all over again." Michael began. "Number one, I remember somethin' else that Aunt Frances told me and I'm findin' out she's good to know."

"I heard she was your best friend."

"And you know it but anyway, she was tellin' me about that scripture in Matthew eighteenth chapter where Jesus was talkin' about how it would be better for you to drown in the sea with a millstone around your neck than to mess over His people."

"I didn't know about that one, where did you say that is?" Marie asked him as she picked up her phone again.

"It's Matthew the eighteenth chapter and the first six verses that she told me to read." Michael said. "And that goes for anybody, not just for where I am."

"Yeah this is somethin' to think about." Marie said a few moments later after finding the scripture and silently reading it.

"So I'm really careful about how I'm handlin' this whole situation and both of us are are really prayin' about us because there's no turnin' back once it's done."

"Does that seem like a hard thing to you?"

"It might seem hard but when you think about it, why would you undo somethin' that God has ordained?" He answered after thinking a moment before speaking.

"You sound like somebody that's been around for a while."

"That's because I've been hangin' around other people that have been around for years and that's helped me to change my thinkin' about a lot of things." He answered. "This time six months ago, I was runnin' away from marriage and commitment and all of that, but when I see men like James and Douglas and the way they love and treat their wives, I had to get up off of that."

"And that's why they were so much help to me the other night when I was there." "They went through some things but they stayed together and that's how they're able to prove that it can be done."

"And we're not so naïve to think that there's not gonna be some issues but who doesn't?"

"Nobody that I know of." Marie said. "Have you ever asked James if they've ever had any racial stuff to deal with?"

"We were talkin' one day and he said most of their problems have been because he's really conscious of not comin' off like he thinks he's better than she is."

"I can see that but it's better to be that way than the other extreme."

"And that was back when they first got married but their problems have come from other people and that can cause some issues too if you don't grow a thick skin."

"Is that what you're doing?"

"I'm startin' to because what difference should it make to somebody else if we crash and burn?"

"It shouldn't but it does and that's when you have to learn how to just be quiet and go on."

"Shut mouth grace?"

"Exactly but I feel like I need to warn you about my mother before she gets here." Marie said after a moment. "She can be really hard to deal with and it's gotten worse since she had that accident."

"Janice said she blames her for that."

"She does and I've told her over and over again not to do that, she's askin' for trouble later on down the line somewhere."

"I asked her why she wants to put that on her and that's when she explained to me about how she came here expectin' to bring her back to D.C. with her."

"And when she found out that Janice wasn't goin' for that, that's when the sparks started to fly between her and Douglas." "It was a mess."

"I heard about that too but she said that whole thing was what helped her to see how real the Holy Ghost is."

"Then I guess it was worth it huh?"

"It was and like Aunt Frances says, God can turn messes into miracles." He said as the waitress came back with their salads.

"I've never heard her say that but I like it, I might have to start thinkin' that way."

"It's like the worse a situation is, the more glory the Lord gets when He brings you out of it." Michael said. "And we really saw that when Terry almost went out of here a couple of months ago."

"Irene told me about that and you can't tell by the way she looks and talks that it ever happened."

"She's a livin' testimony and every chance she gets, she's tellin' people about it."

"I would love to hear it from her because it's always more effective when you get it firsthand, you know what I mean?"

He nodded. "It is, and by this time next year, it'll probably be altogether different with us and I'm sayin' that by faith."

"So how long did it take for you to find a job after you moved up here from St. Louis?" Marie asked a few moments later after he blessed their food.

"It was about two weeks from the day I got here 'til the day I got the phone call that blew my mind." He said, thinking back.

"Then it didn't take long for you to find somethin' else huh?"

"I had to go through some major mind changes before it happened for me and if it wasn't for you know who, I might be still lookin', no kiddin'."

"Your best friend?" Marie asked, amused.

"You know it and I'll tell you why she's probably the reason that it happened like it did." He began. "I had been here for just a week but I had started to feel sorry for myself because things weren't workin' out like I thought they should've been." "I was a egotistical hot mess but God has a way to get pride out of you like nothin' else will."

"Tell me about it but in the long run, you come out better for it."

"I know that now but at the time, all I could think about was that I was runnin' out of money, couldn't find the job I wanted, Janice had kicked me to the curb, the whole ball of wax and I wasn't used to things not goin' my way."

"You would never know that now."

"Believe me, I was that way but to make a long story short, I got pulled over one night for speedin' and ended up downtown with a D.W.I. and that was pretty much my rock bottom."

"Everybody has one." Marie said shaking her head.

"That was on a Sunday night and a couple of days later, I accidently on purpose ended up at her house, feelin' sorry for myself."

"And she probably gave you some tough love didn't she?"

"She knows how to tell you the truth without hurtin' your feelings, and when she told me that pity parties don't get you anywhere, that's when she stopped everything and told me that we were gonna pray about my problems."

"Sounds just like her."

"And by the time she got through with me, I was sittin' there cryin' like a baby; that was the first time I felt the presence of the Lord and that's how I reacted to it."

"So how long was it after that that your job came through?" Marie asked him, fascinated by his testimony.

"That was on a Wednesday, I got that phone call on Friday and I was in shock." He said after thinking for a second. "And there's a part of me that wants to say that it would've happened anyway but after what I experienced that day, I'm not givin' that to anybody or anything except her faith in God."

"You're probably right and I'll be glad when I get to the place where she and Douglas are." "When it comes to faith and things like what you just told me about, they make it look so easy."

"And he learned that from hangin' around with her for the last twenty years." "Did Chris or anybody tell you about Paul's mother-in-law?"

She shook her head. "What happened?"

"Jane's mother was there for dinner a couple of Sundays ago, you know how we get together out there every week after church."

She nodded.

"She told Jane that she had been to the doctor the week before because she had this cough that she couldn't get rid of." Michael said as he opened a sugar packet for his iced tea. "She had a M.R.I. done and they found three malignant tumors on one of her lungs."

"Not good."

"It wasn't, so her and Jane took those five hundred steps over to Chris and James' house; she knew Douglas and Aunt Frances were there and you can probably guess what happened."

"I think I know but I still need to hear about it."

"She took Douglas to the side and let him know what was goin' on with her and Jane told me his answer to that cancer thing was one word." "The first thing he said was "And?"

"Are you serious?"

"She said he shrugged it off like it wasn't that big of a deal." "He told her that we don't have any business bein' intimidated by things like that when Jesus said that we would be able to lay hands on the sick and they would recover."

"And when you put it that way, we shouldn't be." "I was talkin' to somebody at home about faith one night and she said that it's us that make it harder than it has to be."

"And you know it but anyway, she said by the time he got through talkin' to her, she wasn't afraid about it anymore." "They got busy and did what they had to do; Aunt Frances got her little bottle of oil that she keeps in the drawer in their family room and Jane said that they prayed the shortest most powerful prayer that she had ever heard."

"I'm sure it was, I've heard her pray before and like I said, I'll be glad when I get to where they are because they always get what they ask for." Marie said as she anxiously waited for him to finish.

"And you know it, they went back to her doctor a few days later for a follow up appointment from the week before." Michael began. "They took some more X-rays and those tumors that were there the week before were history, gone."

"Oh my God Michael, you just don't hear about things like that everyday." Marie said as she felt the anointing of God behind the testmony.

"I know you don't but that let me know that there's nothin' too hard for God to do." "I've heard that preached but it means more now that we've actually seen it happen."

"Like it was one thing for Abraham and Sarah to see their miracle back in the day but when you see it yourself, it's different."

"It is, she has the before and after X-rays and when she showed 'em to me, it was unreal to have it front of you where you can look at it over and over again and say this is what God did because of faith in Jesus' name." Michael said. "And this thing with Janice and me is no different, I'm not seein' that much right now but it's not about what I see, faith doesn't have to see anything."

"I can tell that you've been goin' to a lot of bible classes because you seem to know what you're talkin' about." Marie told him.

"It's a combination of things that're helpin' me, it's bible class every week and sittin' up under people like Douglas and Aunt Frances, and plain ol' experience, you know what I'm sayin'?"

"I think I do and I'm gonna say this and I don't want you to take it the wrong way." She began.

"Am I in trouble?"

"No honey, you're not in trouble but I did have my reservations about you before today."

110

"I can understand that, you hadn't seen me before Sunday and I'm not so crazy to think that just because I'm buyin' you lunch, that it's all good now." "I wasn't born yesterday and neither were you, let's just keep it real."

"I know what you're sayin' but I can tell that you're on the right track just by some of the things I've heard you say." She said. "And actually, you don't have anything to prove to anybody except Janice and I know that it hasn't been easy."

"It hasn't been easy for her either and I'm glad that she has Douglas to bounce things off of." "She can probably say things to him that she wouldn't feel comfotable sayin' to me and I respect that."

"You mean things that have to do with your relationship?"

He nodded. "She's better off talkin' to him or Aunt Frances because they have the wisdom that neither one of us have yet and if she can get help from them, then so be it." He said as their lunches arrived.

"After talkin' to you, I feel better about mother movin' here because I feel you have what it takes to take her on." Marie told him. "So just remember that you heard it from me first, get yourself ready."...

CHAPTER 5

JULY 5, SUNDAY

"Marie called me right after she got back home Saturday and said that she can't wait to get here." Janice remarked Sunday afternoon at dinner with Sheila, Ruth, James and Douglas at the kitchen table.

"How come you don't sound excited, your mommy's gonna be here with you when you have your baby." Sheila told her.

"I'm sort of glad about that but I think she's gonna give Michael a hard time, that's just the way she is."

"Maybe not, don't talk that up." James said. "Remember what we heard about life and death bein' in the power of your tongue today?" He asked her as he put more meatballs on his plate.

"And you know what, after I heard that, I'm done with sayin' negative stuff." Ruth commented.

"Michael had lunch with Marie last week and he felt like she was warnin' him and that's not good." Janice said.

"But don't you think he'll know how to deal with her?" "He's not a pushover." Sheila said. "Where is he anyway, over at Paul and Jane's?"

"Him and Terry took their plates in there with Aunt Frances, she told me the other day that she likes to sit them down every Sunday to see what they got out of the message."

"And she'll probably have both 'em laughin' and cryin' and all of that, watch it." Sheila said.

"Did she do that with you Douglas?" Ruth asked him.

"I think you already know ma'am, she made sure that I wasn't gonna go back to my junkyard ways." He said after a moment. "And we all know that it's the Holy Ghost that keeps you but she knows how to break it all down to you, especially when you don't quite know what happened to you."

"Sort of like Andre'?"

"Exactly like Andre', when he came to that church, he had no idea what was about to happen to him, but when God sees real repentance in a soul's heart, the Holy Ghost is gonna fall wherever you are."

"Like the day Sara was born?"

"When I got up that day, I really didn't think that I was gonna have to do that but the two experiences are a lot alike." "It didn't matter that Donna was walkin' down the street, when it's time for a baby to come, it's comin', and there's nothin' you can do about it except do what you have to do." "And it's the same way spiritually, you have to be in a place to help people get what God's promised."

"So Douglas tell me this." Sheila began. "What is it that you're doin' or sayin' to people that makes such a difference?"

"A difference in what?" He asked as he poured more iced tea in his glass.

"C'mon Douglas, stop teasin' me."

"I'm not teasin' you ma'am, I can't read your mind so you have to be specific."

"When you and Michael took Andre' back in that room, whatever it was."

"It was the youth pastor's office."

"I mean it was like he was in physical pain because he was so torn up about what was goin' on and it wasn't hardly fifteen or twenty minutes later, here he comes out of there with the Holy Ghost." She said as she recalled the day four weeks earlier.

"It's a matter of bein' able to discern when a person is really serious or just goin' through the motions for some kind of show." He answered. "And if you had been up there and seen and felt what we did, you could've done the same thing."

"Are you sure about that?"

"Can you tell me why you couldn't have?"

"You're puttin' me on the spot Douglas."

"It's just me Sheila Scott, how long have you known me?" "You know I'm harmless don't you?"

"You wouldn't hurt a fly as they say."

"I'm just tryin' to get you to think because we have the same spirit and if you don't have a problem with being out of your comfort zone, there's no reason why you couldn't do the same thing." He said. "But I think I know what you're askin' and that night when we took hm out,he told us about how he found out that Terry would be there and he wanted to hear what she had to say."

"How did he find out?"

"Has Terry told you about Anthony her coworker?"

"She talks about him sometimes."

"He was the one that called the police that night and somehow he hooked up with Andre' and told him that she was gonna be there." Douglas continued. "But it was her testimony that changed everything with him, he didn't have any idea that she was gonna go where she did."

"And that's what made him go up there to talk to her?"

"That was it and that goes to show you how God knows the hearts of people; we have to get out of the habit of lookin' at outward appearances and when the Lord orders things to happen, we need to go with the flow." "He started talkin' and tellin' us about things that we didn't really need to know but if it was helpin' him', then so be it."

"So basically it's about listenin' and lettin' the Lord tell you what to say and do huh?"

"You got it and the soul that God puts in front of you is lookin' to you for answers." "You can't solve all of their problems but you have the responsibility of pointin' them in the direction of where they can get help and it was your Aunt Frances that started me down the right road by sayin' those four words, let God help you."

"Yeah she told us about the night that Irene called her because she didn't know what else to do."

"And that was one of the best things that she's ever done because if she hadn't, I would've been out of here." Douglas said as he remembered his close encounter with suicide. "I had it all planned out; I was waitin' 'til she went to bed and I was goin' out to the car to blow my brains out with a loaded forty-five."

"And that's all she had to say to get you started?" Ruth asked him.

"I didn't have the strength to argue with her and she made it sound so simple that I really didn't have much choice." "I had tried to get high and when that didn't work, I tried to drink that picture out of my head and that just made it worse." He added as he recalled the night of the fatal accident. "She got to me just in time and it had to be the Lord answerin' her prayers, I don't know what else it could've been."

"So you're sayin' all of this to let me know that it depends on the person and how ready they are to let God do what He does." Sheila said.

"That's exactly right, when Terry set him free by forgiving him of all that he put her through, that's what got him to the place where the Lord saw repentance and gave him the Holy Ghost." He answered. "And everybody is different, you have to learn how to let God lead you because He knows just what that soul needs to hear."

"I'm wantin' to know all of this because one of the women that were there that night called me a couple of days ago." Sheila said then.

"From the Second Chance place?"

"You still remember the name of it?" She asked him, surprised.

"Terry's been talkin' about it."

"And when I called the number that's on the business card that I got from Kim, they told me again that they don't have anybody by that name on their staff."

"Your angel." Janice remarked.

"I don't know that a hundred percent but sometimes I still wonder about it." "But anyway, she wants to go with me when I go Thursday night and I just wanted to hear from somebody that knows what they're doin'."

"Just make sure that you pray before you go because you don't have any way of knowin' what you might have to deal with."

"Is that your secret?"

"I'll put it like this, it goes a long way and when you get in the habit of doin' it on a regular basis, you can't help but get results."

Michael told me one time that when he was livin' with you and Irene that he could hear you crashin' the throne every night." Sheila said, amused.

"We're supposed to be prayin' without ceasing so what do you do with that?" He asked, laughing with her.

"Pray without ceasing, that's the book as Aunt Frances says."

"There you go, there's too much stuff goin' on so you can't stop now." He said. "Nothin' is gonna defeat you because that's one of the weapons of our warfare and the devil has to back off because you have the greater spirit."

"Thanks for remindin' me, I knew there was somethin' that I needed to ask you about." She said referring to the incident with Barbara the week before. "Michael told me about that drama last week."

"Is that what he called it?"

"That's my word for it, what's yours?"

"That was just a matter of knowin' how to put those powers of darkness in their place and I'm gonna tell you like I told him and Andre'."

"Was he there too?" Ruth asked him.

"He was and it was a good thing for them to see what the power of the name of Jesus will do when you don't draw back from stuff like that." "He did the right thing by callin' me when he did but there might be a time when I'm not around and he has the same Holy Ghost that I do." "Even demons believe and tremble at the name of Jesus."

"And that spirit had to go huh?"

"Back to hell where it came from." "And I told them not to ever be intimidated by that kind of stuff because fear is what the devil thrives on."

"Has he had any more problems from her?" Sheila asked him.

"He called me again one day last week and she's been okay but she keeps talkin' to him about Phillip but she needs to let go and move on."

"And you might be the only one that can help her with that Douglas." Sheila told him.

"I'll do what I can when she realizes that she needs to move on from what happened twenty years ago because nothin' is gonna bring him back."

"Michael said that she talks to his ashes all of the time so maybe if somebody can talk her into scatterin' 'em somewhere, she might feel better."

"She probably would because that urn sittin' there is a constant reminder to her but she has to get to that place herself."

"But it seems like havin' Andre' around would make a lot of difference to her."

"He said that he's doin' the best he can to be patient with her." "And it's probably a good thing that he's gettin' this experience but that doesn't mean that he doesn't need help with her."

"So you and Michael are sort of on stand by huh?"

"If that's the way you wanna put it, probably so and it's a good thing that Michael is one street away." "He can get over there a lot quicker than I could."

"But it's you that she's obsessed with." She said as James motioned for her not to go there with him.

"She doesn't have any reason to be." He said after a moment as Jane and her mother walked in from outside.

"We just made too many brownies so I'm bringin' half of 'em over here." Jane said as she sat two foil pans down on one of the counters.

"If that's the case, I'm takin' some home." Sheila said as she got up to start clearing the table. "Can't let anything go to waste.

"It's almost like I can't concentrate on anything else and then we hear this message today called How Do you Love." Terry remarked in the family room with Frances and Michael. "I was in shock for a minute."

"And that's what the Lord does because He knows what's on your mind and heart and He'll send you exactly what you need to hear." Frances told her. "I'll never forget a message I heard one Sunday night right after I found out that I was by myself with four kids to raise."

"How old were they when he left?" Michael asked her.

"Donna was six months old and Paul was probably about ten." She said after thinking a moment. "That made Irene and Chris about six and eight and there I was with about fifty dollars to my name, no job and Jesus." She said as she started to laugh at the memory.

"Were you in the house where Michael is now?" Terry asked her as she listened to her every word with fascination.

"That's the one and that's the reason that I didn't sell it to somebody outside of the family." She continued. "Too many memories and that house represents a lot of victories and testimonies for me."

"So I got it for a dollar and I'm tryin' to keep some of the stuff in there the same." Michael said. "Nobody could pay me to change that breakfast nook because that was where I felt the Lord touch me for the first time in my life and you don't forget things like that."

"I learned how to trust God for anything and everything I needed in that place and He did some impossible things that I'll never forget either." "A lot of things went on but the day I watched the water get cut off was when I got to the place where God really started to prove Himself to me." She said, shaking her head. "I stood at the kitchen window and watched 'em do it and all I could do was stand there and say Lord I don't understand, where are you?" She recalled.

"You know what, every time I'm at that window, I'm gonna think about what you just said." Michael said, obviously moved.

"So what did you do?" Terry asked her with sympathy in her voice.

"Honey I couldn't do a thing but stand there and pray in the middle of my pity party." I didn't have any money, I didn't have a car to go out and find a job, etc, etc, and sometimes that's where the Lord wants us so we won't have any choice but to depend on Him." She continued. "I had just started to fix a pot of chicken noodle soup for supper and you can't do that without water so I went over to the refrigerator to see if I had anything I could scrape up to cook without water." She continued with explicit details. "Then I heard the Lord speak to me through my spirit just as clear as I'm talkin' to you right now."

"I'm feelin' chills, this is gonna be good." Michael said then.

"He said go to the faucet and turn it on." She said as she handed Terry a napkin as she noticed her reaction. "And I didn't do it because I thought it was just me thinkin' crazy, they just shut my water off, what good was that gonna do?" "That was me usin' my carnal natural mind instead of bein' obedient so I heard it again; the same thing, go to the faucet and turn it on."

"Oh my God." Terry said as she unashamedly cried into the napkin, knowing what was coming next.

"So I finally went over to the sink and turned one of the faucets on and out it came, hot and cold, just like nothin' had happened." "And I let it run because I thought maybe there was just some left in the pipes and it would eventually stop comin' out." "But it just kept comin' and I went to bathroom to see if the toilet tank would fill back up after I flushed it and sure enough, just like God, it filled up and worked exactly like it was supposed to." She said as she took one of Terry's hands into hers. "And I want both of you to listen to me when I say this." She said pausing. "I don't care what may be comin' down your street to test you, never forget that you have the same God that spoke the world into existance and He's not too big to come and see about you and it doesn't matter what kind of situation you're in."

"That is just crazy." Terry managed to say as she still tried to process what she had just told them.

"Then it came to me that God created every drop of water there is and if He wants to make it happen like that to prove Himself to me, I didn't have a thing to worry about."

"So did the water company ever catch anything behind that?" Michael asked her.

"I never heard a thing but somehow I scraped up twenty dollars to get the bill paid and nothin' else was said about it." "They probably wouldn't have believed it if I had told 'em the truth but so be it, God is in control of His universe and everything that happens down here so we don't have any business worryin' about anything or anybody."

"That's just what I needed to hear, Marie put a bug in my ear about her mother so I have my guard up." Michael said as he emptied his pop can into a glass.

"Then we'll both just have to keep Kathryn in check by askin' the Lord to fight your battles and believe me, He will." Frances said. "I know that from experience too because by the time your big brother showed up at my front door for Irene, I had learned what it meant to intercede for people." "He stepped up my prayer life big time and he had no idea what was goin' on but when God gets ready to change people on your behalf, there's no stoppin' the process."

"How long was it before things started to change?" Michael asked her.

"From that first night 'til the motorcycle accident was probably about two years and every time he'd come and get her, I'd have these images in my mind that were takin' my peace." She said.

"And you weren't supposed to be lettin' that happen."

"Now you're gettin' it son." "And I got that revelation one night when I was stressin' out over these pictures in my mind that were doin' just that." She said. "But then the scripture that says that God hasn't given us the spirit of fear came to my mind, and a sense of peace came over me that I can't explain to this day except that the Lord knows exactly what's goin' on in our minds and He knows how to take care of all of it."

"And that is so good to know because I used to think that it was just the spiritual stuff that the Lord would do things with." Michael said then. "But I was talkin' to somebody at church one night two or three weeks ago about some stuff goin' on at work and he told me to tell the Lord about it and see what happens."

"And it all worked out didn't it?"

"You already know."

"And God knows that if things aren't goin' right with all of these issues and problems that we deal with every day, they start to affect your spiritual life." Frances said. "You can get so worried and stressed about this stuff goin' on down here, that you get distracted from the things that keep you strong." "Then that's when the devil tries to move in on you and one thing leads to another if you're not careful."

"I had somebody at work say somethin' to me the other day that I know came from hell." Terry remarked then. "I used to go to lunch sometimes with one of the cashiers and the last time she wanted me to go with her, I told her that I had somethin' else I had to do and I did." "I wasn't makin' that up; then she told me that I thought I was better than she was just because I'm goin' to somebody's church now." She said laughing a little. "And I wanted to tell her that it's a whole lot deeper than goin' to church; it's about my Holy Ghost tellin' me not to because I can't be involved in the stuff that she does and says any more."

"She wouldn't have understood what you were talkin' about." Michael said.

"That's why I decided to just be quiet and not get into it with her because it could've really been bad." "She's not the type to back down off of anything and then I started to think about how horrible I was before the Lord got hold of me and all I could do was start thankin' God." She said as Michael's phone went off.

"Hey Andre', what's up?" He asked as he stood up. "Everything okay?"

"I hope so, I just talked to my grandmother a minute ago and she asked me to get in touch with Douglas."

"Did she tell you why?"

"She didn't say why she wanted to talk to him but I told her that I'd check with you first to see if he's busy with anything." He answered after a moment. "She lost his business card that he gave her and I didn't feel right givin' her his number but she didn't sound right, you know what I mean?"

"It's not that same stuff like last week was it?"

"She sounded different from that and I'm really tryin' not to bother him any more with her problems."

"Give me a few minutes and I'll have him call you back, tell her that we're workin' on it."

"Sometimes you have to do things that're inconvienient but at the same time, you can't let people bring you down." Douglas remarked as he and Michael sat in his car outside Barbara's house an hour later.

"I get that because somebody had to help us out but where do you draw the line?" Michael asked him.

"You don't draw the line until the Lord says so and sometimes it means doin' things that are outside of your comfort zone." He answered.

"Does this fit that description?" He asked him as he nodded towards her house.

"It's not that it's uncomfortable but when things that happened so long ago keep showin' back up and remindin' you about where you came from, it's not easy to deal with." He said after a moment. "And if it wasn't for the way this all happened, I probably wouldn't be as involved but none of this was an accident."

"She probably has no idea what she's doin' but all you can do is go in here and see what's on her mind." Michael said. "And when I talked to Andre', he made sure I knew that he got rid of the gun she had."

"I'm not worried about that but it was probably a good thing that he did; she's too unstable to have a pistol in the house." Douglas said as they got out of the car.

"Man I hope you don't mind comin' all the way over here but she won't let it alone." Andre' remarked as he met them on the porch. "I keep tellin' her over and over again that she needs to get out of the past because she's makin' herself sick thinkin' about my father all of the time." He added as they noticed the effect that she was having on him.

"Maybe we need to take a ride, c'mon." Michael told him as he motioned him towards his car while Douglas went into the house.

"You came, come over here and talk to me." Barbara told him as she sat blankly staring at the t.v.

"What's on your mind?" He asked her as he turned the volume down with the remote.

"I talked to Phillip again last night and he-

"Okay, I'm stoppin' you right there ma'am." He said, interrupting her before she could finish her sentence. "I'm not here to listen to that kind of talk because he's been gone for twenty years." He added with a firm but calm voice. "I don't know what you think you're hearing but you'll be a lot better off when you start to concentrate on who is living, do you understand what I'm saying to you?" He asked as he made intense eye contact with her.

She nodded slightly without speaking.

"Do you know how you're makin' Andre' feel?"

"I'm only tryin' to let him know how his father was because he never had the chance to meet him." "You took him away that night and it's so unfair." She finally spoke, close to tears.

"Is that what you think happened?" He patiently asked her. "Because if it is, I'll tell you about it this one time and it's up to you whether you believe it or not but it really doesn't matter." He added as he began to reluctantly recall the night of the accident in his mind.

She nodded again while reaching out for him as her means to somehow connect with her son.

"There were six of us leavin' a party around ten or eleven o'clock on a Friday night." He began. "Phil wanted to stop off at a crack house to pick up some more drugs because we were all high and he was runnin' out." He continued as he remembered every detail. "We were on motorcycles and he and I were sharin' a joint when he told me he'd meet me there, and those were his last words." He remarked as he took a handkerchief from his shirt pocket. "He took off and a few seconds later, I watched him lose control and hit a telephone pole headon and he wasn't wearin' a helmet." He added, shaking his head as he visualized the scene that nearly caused him to end his own life.

"So it's true that-

"Yes ma'am, that part is true, I know where you're goin' and I don't think that you need to hear about the details that I saw that night so we'll just leave it right there." He managed to say. "And you need to know that it was the Lord that allowed Andre' to show up almost out of nowhere; He did that so you wouldn't be alone for the rest of your life and even though Phillip is gone, you have his son and that's the next best thing." He concluded as she seemingly began to experience a significant breakthrough after hearing his traumatic eyewitness account.

"I'm so sorry that you had to see that but I feel better now that I know exactly what happened." Barbara said through falling tears.

"Has this been on you for twenty years?"

"Nobody has been able to tell me exactly what went on until now." "All they told me was that it was an accident on his motorcycle but I always wondered how that could be, he was always so careful."

"That doesn't make any difference when you're drugged up like we were that night." "That stuff messes up your mind and makes you feel like nothin' can hurt you but if it helps any, he didn't suffer because it happened so fast." Douglas said. "And all of that needs to be shut down because there's enough goin' on right now that needs to be taken care of."

"What do you mean?"

"I think it would do both you and Andre' a lot of good if you do somethin' different with this urn over here that's a constant reminder of what both of you lost." Douglas suggested to her. "He's really tryin' to have a relationship with you because he knows that you don't have any other family besides him, but it's not easy for him to do that because you've been so caught up with his father who's not even here anymore."

"Doesn't he know how much he's changed things for me?" She asked him.

"I'm not sure if he does, have you ever told him that?"

"I thought that he knew and he's such a nice young man so I would hate to hurt his feelings because of something I said." She spoke with heartfelt sincerity. "Do you think he's upset with me?"

"I don't think he's upset but he seems to be a little frustrated because every time he comes by to see about you, he has to hear about his father who is not here anymore." He said again with purposeful emphasis.

"What did he tell you when he called you today?"

"He called Michael and he gave me the message that you wanted to talk but it's not about me." "You need to sit down with him and see where his head is because if you don't, he might just stop tryin', you get what I'm sayin'?"

"Where is he now?"

"He left with Michael a few minutes ago, they probably went over there to his house."

"I didn't mean to run him away."

"But that's what happens when you get so focused on yourself and your issues." "He's really tryin' to help you but if you keep remindin' him about how he grew up without his father and how unfair it all seems to you, you're pushin' him away and that's the last thing he needs."

"I try to go over there at least a couple of times a week and it's the same thing over and over again." "Andre' remarked with Michael as they sat on his porch. "And I hope that Douglas can do somethin' about that because I respect her too much to tell her what I'm really thinkin.'" He admitted to him.

"I can almost guarantee you that he's over there takin' care of business with her." Michael told him, laughing a little. "You saw what happened last week didn't you?"

"And I haven't heard any more of that craziness either." "Andre' said. "And don't get me wrong, I understand that it hurt and all of that but none of that kind of talk is gonna bring him back; I just want her to know how much the Lord can help her if she would just get out of herself."

"Have you told her about what happened to you?"

"I've tried to explain it to her but you know how that goes, until it happens to you, there's just no way to understand it."

"Tell me about it but all you can do is keep lovin' her even if she's gettin' under your skin because you're all she has."

"So has she known Douglas all of this time?"

"He told me that he met her maybe once or twice when him and your father were friends twenty or twenty one years ago." Michael began. "Then when she happened to be sittin' on her porch when

125

Douglas had to deliver his sister-in- law's baby, she saw him and remembered who he was."

"After all of that time, she remembered him?"

"It sounds a little bizarre that he would just happen to be in that predicament but it was all meant to be." "And that's why he feels like he has to hang tough with her, that wasn't a coincidence." Michael said. "And then for you to show up the way you did, it has to be the Lord from start to finish."

"So he's not upset because I've had to call him two weeks straight about her?"

"No way, I've learned since I moved up here that you do what you have to do when it comes to people that really need help like she does." He said after a moment. "And you never know when it'll be you that needs somebody to come and see about you, I learned that the hard way." Michael said as he heard a text coming from Douglas then.

"Everything ok?" Andre' asked.

He nodded. "They're walkin' over here, he said to sit tight."

"He talked to me and said that I might be pushin' you away because I was talkin' about your father too much." Barbara remarked with Andre' in the kitchen fifteen minutes later. "Is that true baby?"

"I mean I know that it was an awful thing that happened to him but I'm ready to see you move on from all of that." Andre' said then close to tears. "You can't bring him back and I want you to have the same thing that changed my life around." He said in a pleading way.

"Is that why you wanted me to go to church with you a couple of weeks ago?" Barbara asked him.

"I wanted you to see the place where God gave me another chance after I got myself in trouble." He said. "And you can be healed from all of these bad feelin's that you've been holdin' on to for all of this time." He said as Michael and Douglas came in from outside.

"Are you doin' any better Miss Barbara?" Michael asked her then as he opened the refrigerator.

"Thank you for comin' to see about me because I think things might get better for me now." She responded as Douglas sat down at the table next to Andre' across from her.

"And the best way for you to get over is to let God help you through people that love and care about you." He told her. "None of us understand why things happened like they did but the bottom line is you're still here for a reason and the Lord isn't done with you yet."…

July 8
Wednesday

"We'll have you come back in another two weeks for another sonogram so we can confirm what it appears to be and we'll go over your options with you then." Chris' physician told she and James after informing them that she was carrying conjoined twins. "They are obviously identical because they are in one yolk sac as you can see here." He added as he pointed them out on the screen. "And of course it's too early to know what the gender is but at this point, you still have the option of terminating this pregnancy."

"No that's not an option." James immediately spoke then as he and Chris stared at the screen together. "That's not happenin'." He added with finality.

"And you're on the same page with that decision?" He asked Chris.

"There's no way that we're doin' that." She managed to say as they continued to look at the screen as the technician continued to examine the two images that appeared to be joined at the chest.

"Then we have to inform you that if these babies survive, they will have a lot of problems that will take a lot of surgeries to correct." He continued. "We don't know yet if they share any organs but there is a good chance that we'll be able to see more in two weeks when you're farther along."

"Is there anything else that you think we should know about this?" James asked him as he noticed Chris begin to lose her composure.

"If you happen to change your minds about this, don't hesitate to let us know and we can take care of it as soon as possible."

"That's not an option." James said again as he helped Chris to sit up. "We're takin' this one day at a time and we'll be back in two weeks."

"If you had come over here and told me this a month ago I would've been in a panic, but this is gonna be allright James." Jane told him two hours later as he sat at the island in the kitchen after showing her the sonogram pictures.

"We know it is but you have to admit that this is not a joke to your natural mind, you know what I mean?" James said.

"I know it's not but that's what we have to get out of honey, this is just a test of our faith and when this is all said and done, you and Chris are gonna have a testimony out of this world, you hear me?"

"I hear you." He said as he folded the pictures up.

"I know Douglas was the first one you called wasn't he?" Jane asked him as she started filling the dishwasher.

"You know me too well."

"And we know that it'll be the Lord that is gonna do this work but He's put him in a position to keep everybody level headed, you know?" "Him and mother need to write a book together about all of the things that God has done through them and I'm dead serious when I say that."

"I know you are and you can probably guess what his reaction was when I told him what was goin' on." James said. "He said one of two things are goin' on and when I thought about it, it made a lot of sense."

"It always does."

"Either they've made a misdiagnosis or the Lord has allowed it to be just to let us know that this is a light thing for Him to do."

"And it is and I wish I could tell you how much my faith has grown since we saw the Lord take care of my mother's issue." "It's like, bring it on, nothin' is impossible when you believe God."

"And both of us know that that's so easy to say, we have to keep it real Jane." James said.

"I know we do but when we're dealin' with stuff like this, sometimes the Lord is showin' us just where our faith levels are and where we need to come up." Jane said as she sat down across from him. "What did mother say when you told her about it?"

"She told us not to panic because God is in control." He said after a moment as he recalled her initial reaction. "And that's when Chris lost it and she made me almost lose it because I have a hard time when I see her goin' through, you know what I mean?"

"Of course, she's your wife and it would be somethin' wrong if you weren't feelin' it."

"And I'm not used to seein' her lose it over anything, she'll hold it together for all of us when somethin' happens but this is different." He said. "And it helps to know that we're not in this by ourselves, Douglas told me that these were everybody's babies and we're gonna pull 'em through, case closed in other words."

"Now you're gonna make me lose it James." Jane remarked after hearing him repeat Douglas' words of encouragement.

"That's the way he put it, he said your babies belong to the whole family and it's time to get busy and act like it."

"By takin' the Lord at His word and keepin' it simple." Jane said. "After my mother's experience, I don't pray the same way that I used to and I'm findin' out that when you start thankin' God in advance for doin' what you're askin' Him to do, that's believin' before you see and that's the faith that He's lookin' for."

"Before I came over here, I was givin' Chris and mother some space because I could tell that she couldn't wait to do what she does best."

"And that doesn't have anything to do with you, it's a mother daughter thing so don't get your feelings hurt." She added. "But what you can do to help her get through this is to really step it up when it comes to the other kids, she shouldn't have to do much of anything." "And since my kids are growin' up and gettin' really independent, I can come help out too, don't hesitate to call me over there."

"That's good to know but I'm tryin' not to think too far ahead with this because if I do, too many scenarios come to my mind and I refuse to go there."

"And we're with you so don't ever feel like this is just you and Chris' thing because it's not." She said. "And when you bring 'em home in January, this will be another testimony that you'll be talkin' about for years, mark my words.".…

JULY 9, THURSDAY

"I need both of you to fill out this registration form that all visitors have to complete when they come to "My Second Chance." The receptionist told Terry and Sheila Thursday evening. "Then after we do a background check on you, we give you a passcode to get in the building and the only stipulation that we have is that you let us know three days in advance that you're coming." She added as they took the paperwork from her. "You have an hour to visit and if by chance you might need more time, let us know what your plans are because we have to be really careful about the way things are maintained here." "The families that we have here are in the process of starting their lives over and we can't take the chance of any setbacks because of old relationships that caused them to be here in the first place."

"So everything is really confidential in other words." Sheila remarked.

"It has to be because these ladies are here for their own protection, they've been in abusive relationships and we help them to make a new start in life." She answered. "How did you find out about this place, it's very unusual for Second Chance to have people from the outside to visit us like you are."

"We met a lady at a restaurant about a month ago and she gave us this card." Terry said as she showed it to her.

"I called to see if she worked here but nobody knew anything about her." Sheila spoke up. "She told us that her name was Kim and the forst and last time that we heard from her."

"She might've been somone that has a relative here but I can look into that for you if you would like to talk to her again."

"Don't worry about it, the main thing is that we know that you're here now and when you get everything checked out with us, we'll be back."

"If I didn't know better, that background check would be worryin' me but I'm not goin' there." Terry remarked half an hour later as they sat in her car at Douglas and Irene's house.

"If that's the only thing on your record, that probably wouldn't be enough to make a difference." Sheila said, referring to her arrest in St. Louis a few months before.

"And when I think about that now, it's like I had to be out of my mind to let myself live like that."

"It's not that you were out of your mind, it's that you didn't know that there was another way to do it." Sheila remarked. "And that goes for all of us but when you're in it, the devil is not gonna let you see the flip side of stuff."

"You got that right but I have to look at it as a way to help somebody else." She said after a moment. "I mean if I hadn't gone through some of what I did, I wouldn't be able to say that I know firsthand about what God can do."

"And you just don't know what this might lead to, it wasn't any accident that woman showed up that day at Gringo's." Sheila said, shaking her head. "And we get in trouble sometimes tryin' to figure stuff out instead of just trustin' the Lord with things like this."

"So you think it might not make any difference?"

"If the Lord wants you there for somebody, it's not gonna matter what might show up on your background check because He's in control." Sheila said with authority and confidence.

"Has anything like this ever happened to you before?"

"Not exactly like this but I remember fillin' out an application and lyin' about the experience I had so I could get this job that was payin' about fifteen dollars an hour." Sheila began. "This was probably about five or six months before the Lord gave me the Holy Ghost and I was pretty much out of control." She said, laughing a little.

"How long ago was this?"

"Close to six years ago." She said thinking back. "So when they finally called me to come in for a interview, they read over my resume and all of that and by this time, I couldn't lie about it anymore." "I wasn't about to get in trouble by lyin' again so I decided to come clean and tell 'em that some of the things that I had put on there just weren't true and I just knew that would be it, I was history."

"And they hired you anyway?"

"They did and I remember prayin' about it before I went to the interview and you know what they told me?"

Terry shook her head in anticipation of her answer.

"The guy that was interviewin' me told me that I probably wouldn't have been hired if all of that stuff that I made up was true because I would've been over qualified." Sheila said. "And I almost lost it right then and there because I was so shocked but that taught me that it just doesn't matter about stuff like that when you have God on your side."

"That's crazy how all of that worked out."

"It is but when you read in the scripture that says all things work together for our good to them that love God, it's not so crazy if you believe that." Sheila said as she typed in Romans 8:28 on her phone for her to read in its entirety.

"And we know that all things work together for good to them that love God, to them who are called according to his purpose." Terry read half a minute later.

"And if we really believe that like we should be, we shouldn't be surprised when stuff works out even when it looks like it shouldn't."

"This is so good to know, I had no idea that was in here." She said as she stared at the scripture, reading it over again.

"Just keep comin' to bible class and talkin' to people like Aunt Frances and you'll find out about a lot of other scriptures that'll help you get over." Sheila said. "But we're gonna pray that it won't even be an issue and what God starts He's gonna finish; He doesn't do things halfway."

"Douglas told me that one night when we were talkin' about somethin' else a couple of weeks ago."

"It's true and I've got another scripture about that too." Sheila said as she began to look for Phillipians 1:6 on her phone. "Read this one and tell me what you think it means." She added as she handed it back to her.

"Being confident of this very thing, that he which hath begun a good work in you will perform it until the day of Jesus Christ." She read, tears falling down her face as the Word of God spoke directly to her fears and apprehensions.

"It sounds like whatever He starts, He'll finish it." She managed to say.

"In a nutshell as Aunt Frances likes to say." "He started this thing with you when you met Kim that day and one thing lead to another and He's not gonna let somethin' like this background check get in the way of what He has planned for you to do for these people at the shelter."

"Do you think that they're still there?"

"I still have their names and numbers if you wanna put 'em in your phone and try to call and let 'em know that we haven't forgotten about comin'." She offered.

"It was three or four of 'em wasn't it?"

"It was and maybe if I call two and you call two, it'll work out better." She suggested as she began to search through the contacts list on her phone.

"Sounds like a plan, I'll let you know how it goes."...

JULY 11, SATURDAY

"There's one part of my mind that's tellin' me things would be better if I would have a miscarriage and then there's the other side that's sayin' have you lost your mind?" Chris remarked with Irene and Douglas out on their screened porch Saturday afternoon.

"That's the way it always is, you're in a warfare and it's gonna take everything you have to make it through this but you will." Douglas said with finality. "By this time next year, you're gonna look back on what you're goin' through now and you'll probably be wonderin' why you were thinkin' like this."

"I hope so because right now, it's like I'm in the middle of a fog and I know good and well that it can't stay this way." She admitted. "We have seven other kids that don't have a clue about what's goin' on and we can't start slackin' with them because of this."

"I don't think you're slackin' just because you're dealin' with this, you can't just act like nothin' is goin' on." Irene told her. "And do they even know that they're comin'?"

"Patti just came out and asked me the other day about why I was lookin' different and I'm like, is she payin' that much attention?"

"How old is she, eight?"

She nodded. "So I just went on and told her but I didn't tell her that it was twins again." She said, shaking her head.

"They'll find out but what you don't want to do is start stressin' them out just because you're worried about it." Douglas told her. "Like I told James when he first told me, this is where it stops." "We can't be worried and fearful that this or that is gonna happen because that's a sure sign of mistrust and doubt about the power of God." He continued. "And at this point, all we can do is what we know is right and whatever the Lord does or doesn't do, we have to learn that He's not gonna give you any more than what you can bear." He said as she began to react to his words with silent and healing tears before they came to her side together for comfort and support.

As they began to intercede for her, she began to experience a sense of peace that came from the "effectual prayer of the righteous". The burden that she had been carrying since the day of the diagnosis inexplicably began to fade and was replaced by a surge of faith that the situation was under the control of Almighty God.

"Tell James that we need to have a conversation some time tomorrow." Douglas told Chris half an hour later as he walked her out to her van.

"That would probably do him a lot of good because I'm startin' to think that he's blamin' himself for this and I've tried to tell him that this is nobody's fault and to stop it, you know what I mean?"

"The last time I checked, it takes two people to make a baby." He said as he opened the door for her. "Is he serious or what?"

"He hasn't actually come out and said that but I know how he thinks Douglas." She said as she fastened her seat belt. "And I love him to death but he's got some issues." She added as she got tissues from the box next to her on the seat.

"C'mon back in here, you don't need to be drivin.'" Douglas told her as he opened the door back up.

"You don't have to say any more than you want to but we can't let this eat at you like this." Irene told her a few minutes later in the livingroom. "Douglas went to call James and he thinks that he needs to talk to you together."

"Is he gonna have him come over here?" Chris asked her as they sat down on the sofa.

"That's what he said and I know that James wanted you to have some time to yourself away from the kids for a minute but he doesn't feel like this can wait because it's stressin' you out more than it needs to be."

"It's just a little too much goin' on at one time." Chris said after thinking a moment. "He told me the other day that he's thinkin' about goin' into business on his own because of some stuff that he's heard on his job." She said as Douglas came in then.

"James is on his way." He said as he sat down. "But 'til he gets here, you need to know that this is the time to get things out in the open because when you hold stuff in, they won't get any better." "We love you too much to sit back and not do anything about what's goin' on so just sit tight for a minute or two."

"It's a matter of not knowin' where this is goin' and all of us know what God can do, that's not the issue." James remarked an hour later, back out on the porch with Douglas and Chris.

"In other words you're gettin' caught up in what you think may not happen."

"I'm keepin' it real and I'm tryin' to get myself together for what might be, simple as that."

"Does that feel like doubt to you?"

"It does and I don't like it but it is what it is and ever since we found this out, I'm havin' a fight in my mind about how to deal with my doubts." James admitted. "And as her husband, that's not gonna work." He added. "She can't go through this by herself but right now, that's what it's feelin' like."

"You're feelin' guilty because you don't think you're doin' enough." Douglas said in effort to get an understanding of his thoughts.

"That's pretty much it."

"Honey I don't know what else we can do except believe the Lord about this and maybe we're goin' through this to let us know how off the mark we are, you know what I mean?"

"I can see that, maybe so." He conceded.

"But have you thought about that the other way around Chris?" Douglas asked her.

"How do you mean?" She asked after a moment.

"Sometimes we go through things so we can see what's actually possible when we're believin' God like we're supposed to be." He said. "And that's not any new revelation, we all know it but sometimes we need reminders and get hit with a red hot test and we find out what we're made of."

"Are we gonna be able to look back on this and wonder how we got over?" She asked, as she managed to laugh a little.

"That's pretty much up to you and you might be surprised at how much your attitude about things like this affect your outcome." "This is a light thing with God and when you get to the place where you don't have any doubt that He'll do exactly what He said He would, we're gonna see another miracle." He added with confidence and faith.

"You sound just like mother." Chris said, wiping her face as James put his arm around her.

"That's what happens when you sit under somebody that has seen the Lord do impossible things over and over again, it can't help but get in your spirit." He said. "And from day one when they showed me in the scripture that He would give me the Holy Ghost if I just asked and then it happens a few nights later, that was when I started to take God

at His word; He can't lie and He can't fail and this is no different."
He said as he stood up and approached them. "And James it's time
for you to lay your hands on your wife and heal your children in the
name of Jesus." He told him as he gently guided his free hand to her
"middle" as they began to simultaneously began to pray the prayer of
faith to move the mountain that was in front of them.

As they reacted to the unmistakable anointing and presence of
God, a sense of peace and approval for their trust in the Word of God
that proclaims that nothing shall be impossible to them that believe,
began to overwhelm them. The spirits of doubt, fear and unbelief had
no choice but to flee and bow to the name of Jesus that has all power
over any condition or situation.

"Believe that this is done?" Douglas asked them after they had
boldly come to the throne of grace, anticipating a good report as
reward of their faith.

Chris nodded then through her tears as James continued to
comfort and support her.

"Then this is the time to thank and praise God in advance for
what we'll be seeing because all of us know about His faithfulness."
Douglas told them. "We don't know when and how we're gonna hear
about your good report but it's just a matter of time."…

JULY 12, SUNDAY

"I called you because I want you to help me do somethin' that I
can't do by myself." Barbara remarked Sunday afternoon with Andre'.

"I would've come sooner but I was busy with somethin' at church
and I couldn't get away." He told her as they hugged. "What's goin' on?"

"I can't stop thinkin' about some of the things that Douglas told
me last week when he was here." She began. "He said that it would
probably be good if I did somethin' with this urn sittin' here on
this table." She added as she tried to keep herself from losing her
composure.

"What's on your mind?" He asked her as he sat down next to her.

"I wanted to ask you about it first because this was your father." She managed to say. "I want to go out to Easter Lake to scatter his ashes so that I can start my life over again and I can't do that if I see this every day remindin' me of what I used to have."

"But do you feel comfortable doin' that yourself or is it because we think you should?" He asked her. "If you don't wanna really do that, you can put this somewhere else in the house where you won't see it every day." He suggested.

"But if I know that it's here, I'll be right back in the same place that I don't want to be in anymore." She said after a moment. "And it really helps that I have part of him here through you but I can't forget the way that he looked me in my eyes and told me that I needed to concentrate on who is still alive."

"The man don't play because he knows how close he came to dyin' himself." Andre' told her. "And he didn't talk to you like that to make you feel bad but he wanted you to understand how much better off you'll be if you just let go and let God bless you."

"I know that He blesses me all of the time and He gave you to me to take Phillip's place." She remarked.

"Is that the way it feels to you?"

"What else could be the reason?" "I've been thinkin' about it and it feels like I'm supposed to do this; I haven't been able to sleep because of it." She admitted.

"Did you know that I've been prayin' about this?" Andre' asked her after a moment.

"Does this mean that much to you?" She asked him in shock at his response.

"It does because it hurts me to see you so caught up in what can't be changed Gram." He said. "And it hasn't always been that way with me, I got in trouble a couple of months ago and if it wasn't for other people that cared enough about me to help me, I wouldn't be sittin' here talkin' to you like this." Andre' said as he recognized the opportunity to witness to her.

"What kind of trouble Andre'?"

"That's not really important right now but what matters is that God knows how much this whole thing has hurt you and that's why things happened like they did." He said as he became emotional at the thought of how the Lord ordered the series of events that occurred to bring them together. "Douglas told me how he ended up out there in front of your house to deliver a baby and you recognized him after twenty years." He continued in amazement.

"I remember that day." She managed to say as she noticed how he had been affected by the circumstances that eventually led to the salvation of his soul.

"And he still thinks about that night sometimes but he doesn't let it mess him up like it did when it first happened." "And it was because of what went down with my father that he found out what God will do when you let Him help you."

"Do you think the same thing could happen to me?"

"I know it can and if you feel like you're ready to do this, we don't have to wait." Andre' told her. "I think this would be a good start for you." He added as he got up and walked towards the copper colored urn and gently picked it up before taking it out to his car without any further conversation.

"Do you think that Douglas would want to go with us?" Barbara asked him a minute later as he came back into the house for her.

"I don't think it would be a good idea to bother him anymore about this because he's been here the last two weeks." Andre' said as he helped her to stand up.

"But Phillip was his friend-

"I know he was but I can't keep callin' him over here when it's not really necessary." "Do you think that's fair to him?" He asked her as he patiently waited for her answer while leading her towards the front door.

"But I don't think he would mind if you call him just one more time." She persisted.

"I'll tell you what Gram." He began. "After we get back, you can call him yourself and tell him about what God helped you to do." He suggested to her.

She nodded as she reluctantly agreed while he closed the door behind them.

"Am I doin' the right thing?" She asked him a few minutes later in the car as he found the directions to Easter Lake on his phone.

"Yes ma'am I do and I'm proud of you for doin' this, did you know that?"

She didn't answer but began to stare ahead of her in deep thought.

"And I think that you're gonna feel a lot better after you get it done." He told her.

"Would you be upset with me if I changed my mind?"

"I would be disappointed with you but I couldn't be upset about it because I know this isn't easy for you." He answered her with understanding and patience. "But if you want things to change for you, you have to let things go that are holdin' you back."

"Is that what you did?"

"I had to because if I didn't, I would probably still be messed up in my mind about some things that happened." He said as he thought back to the day he came to a place of repentance after hearing Terry's testimony that was instrumental to his deliverance.

"Are you gonna tell me about what happened?"

"It's not somethin' that I need to talk about because it's in my past and I want you to experience the same thing that I did." He answered her after a moment.

"Can I think about it some more before we go?" She asked him.

"Okay and while you're doin' that, I'm gonna take a walk around the block and I'll be back in ten minutes." He told her as he fought the urge to respond with impatience and frustration with her.

"She called you because she wants your help and now she can't make up her mind about it?" Douglas asked Andre' on the phone a minute later after deciding to call him for his assistance with Barbara.

"She said that she couldn't sleep because of somethin' you said to her last week." He began as he allowed a spirit of peace to overcome his temptation to walk away from Barbara and her continuing issues.

"I didn't talk to her to keep her up at night."

"I know you didn't but you must've said somethin' to make her think because she was ready to go and finally get rid of that urn but somethin' is holdin' her back." "We were in the car about to go out to Easter Lake, then she asked me if I would be upset if she changed her mind about it and that's when I left her by herself for a minute."

"Alright son, everything is under control, I'm glad you called me." Douglas told him.

"I would've called you sooner but I don't wanna keep botherin' you with her problems." He explained.

"But here's what you have to remember Andre." Douglas began. "There's not a one of us that hasn't had some kind of issue or problem that we couldn't handle by ourselves so it doesn't bother me when you call, never forget that." "Where would we be if somebody hadn't taken the time for us and I know that she's not easy to deal with but this is your grandmother and you're pretty much all she has."

"Yes sir."

"But at the same time, if she's not really ready to do that, don't try to force her into it because that might do more harm than good."

"When she called and asked me to come by, I didn't have any idea that's what she wanted." "She said that she couldn't do it by herself then all of a sudden, she said she wasn't sure about it and she wanted to think about it some more."

"Then let her do just that because the last thing you want to happen is for her to come back and blame you later on and then you'd really have a mess." Douglas told him. "You don't want to undo any good that you've done with her and as much as both of us would like to see her let go and move on, it's got to come from her."

"When you put it like that I'm glad that I didn't lose it with her because I was about to." He admitted.

"Is that when you decided to call?"

"I could feel myself about to go off on her but then somethin' told me not to."

"And you know what that was don't you?"

"Yes sir, I know that it was the Holy Ghost that stopped me from doin' somethin' that I would've been sorry for later on."

"And you have to keep lettin' the Lord lead you if you want her to see what He's doin' for you." "It's not so much what you say to her but it's how you allow your spirit to keep you doin' the right thing that will affect her." Douglas concluded. "Where is she now?"

"I left her in my car in front of the house because I had to get away from the situation for a minute." "I'm just walkin' around the block to give her some time to think about it some more."

"Maybe you need to head back over there." "And whatever happens, just remember to let the Lord use you and you might be surprised at what you can do when you get out of yourself."

"Yes sir." He said again out of respect for his words of wisdom and instruction that had helped him to better understand his role in Barbara's life. "And whatever happens, I'll call you back to let you know what went down."

"Can we go now?" Barbara asked him five minutes later as he came back to the car where she was patiently waiting on him to return.

"Yes ma'am." He said in the midst of his shock and surprise at her changed demeanor. "But I don't want you feel any kind of pressure about this and if you're not a hundred percent, we don't have to go."

"But if we keep talkin' about it, it'll never happen." "Let's go." She told him.

"Is this a good place for you?" Andre' asked her half an hour later as they approached an area of the lake that was secluded away from the other activity of the surrounding park.

She nodded as she slowly opened the door with her free hand while carefully holding the twenty year old urn with the other.It was then that he noticed how she was shaking nervously at the prospect of what she was about to do.

"Gram why don't you let me carry this down there for you, you don't want this to spill out do you?" Andre' asked her as he carefully steadied her hand.

"You can." She said as she slowly let go of the urn as she began to quietly cry tears of grief, knowing that this action was the end of an era and the beginning of a new season for her.

"Do you want me to go back to the car and wait on you to finish?" Andre' asked her a minute later as they stood behind a guardrail that overlooked the lake while she tightly clutched the urn.

"If you leave me here by myself, I might change my mind, that's why I wanted you to come with me." "And this was your father, you're a part of this too." She added with pleading in her voice.

"Okay, this is what we'll do." Andre' told her then as he once again became frustrated with her continued indecision. Then at the same time, he began to recall Douglas' instruction to allow the Lord to use him as it came to him to take control of the situation.

She didn't speak but began to listen to him as he attempted to lead her one small step at a time. Then as she heard Andre' begin to quietly pray on her behalf for strength to release what was but no longer is, her understanding began to come open when she listened to his words to the Lord in her behalf. It was then that she allowed him to physically place his hand over hers and helped her take the top from the urn and slowly tip it over to allow the ashes to fall out into the water below them.

"C'mon Gram, you're doin' good." Andre' told her as she felt the tension that she had been feeling dissipate as they watched Phillip's remains float across the slow moving lake out of sight in a matter of minutes.

"How do you feel?" He asked her as they turned around to start back to his car.

"Can we sit right here for a minute?" She asked him as she noticed a nearby picnic table.

"Okay, we can do that." Andre' said as he began to call Douglas again while Barbara slowly sat down.

"Who are you callin'?' She asked him as she took a tissue from her dress pocket.

"I told Douglas that I would call him back when we got done with everything and he'll probably wanna talk to you."

"Please?" She asked him as her demeanor changed at the thought of his willingness to take time with her.

"Barbara?" He asked her half a minute later after Andre' set his phone down on the table and put it on speaker.

"I'm right here." She managed to say as she became overcome at the sound of his now familiar voice that had ministered to her since the day of their "chance" meeting two months before.

"Do you feel like talkin' to me about how you feel now?" Douglas asked her.

"I'm glad that you told me to do it because I think I'll feel better when I go back home tonight." She said with fumbling words.

"I might've suggested it but you were the one that made up your own mind and we don't want you to feel like that you were forced into it." He told her.

"If Andre' wasn't here to help me, I would've changed my mind but he wouldn't let me." She said while simultaneously crying and laughing.

"So what does that tell you hon?"

"I'm just so thankful that I still have a part of Phillip that's still with me."

"And the way that all of that came together tells us that the Lord has been mindful about you all of this time." "What you did today was just symbolic because he's been gone for over twenty years but now that you've let go, God will take you to another level if you allow Him to."

"The Holy Ghost?" She asked him after a moment.

"Absolutely." "Has Andre' talked to you about what happened to him?"

"I've been to church with him a couple of times and I've heard about that."

"And that's a good thing, don't stop goin' because the more you go, the more you'll learn about what the Lord has for you when you believe Him." Douglas told her. "Can you promise me that you're gonna move forward and let God help you?"

"I think I'll be able to now." She said after a moment.

"That's what we like to hear and don't hesitate to call if you need us for anything." "I know Andre probably checks up on you pretty often but if he's not available, you still have my number don't you?"

Without answering, she got up from the table and started back to Andre's car, overwhelmed at the love and concern that she was feeling from the two of them.

"I think she needed to be by herself for a minute, she went back to the car." Andre' explained to Douglas then.

"I can understand that but whatever you do, don't try to get deep with her and try to quote a lot of scriptures that you don't have a lot of understandin' about." He told him "You're doin' the right thing by havin' her come to church with you and as long as you keep lovin' and understanding her, the Lord will do the rest."

"That's about the same thing that Michael told me the other day." He said in agreement.

"And we don't tell you that to discourage you but right now, she needs your love and support more than anything." "When she sees that you're doin' more than a lot of talkin', the rest will fall into place."

"Yes sir."

"So go and see about her and we'll just take it one day at a time." Douglas concluded. "You did good."…

CHAPTER 6

JULY 16, THURSDAY

"When I told Marie that both of us would be here, she got so excited. Janice remarked with Michael as they waited on Kathryn and Marie at the airport Thursday evening.

"She didn't think you'd be here by yourself did she?"

"She thought maybe Douglas would be here like last time but she wanted her to meet you right away."

"So that's why I'm here instead of him huh?"

"Somethin' like that." Janice said then after a moment. "And I told Marie to ask her not to start anything with you."

"I'm expectin' her to and ever since you told me that she was movin' here, I've been prayin' about me and the way that I come off to her."

"Are you sorry that she decided to do this?"

"I'm not because I understand why she wants to be here for you but I don't want her to stress you out either." Michael said. "I can take stuff from people but I've heard about what happened right before I got here and it didn't sound like anybody's joke."

"It wasn't but we got stuff straightened out and if she wants to go back there, I'm not goin' with her." Janice said. "I have too much to do to get ready for the baby to be goin' backwards with her."

"What else do you have to do?"

"I made a list that Chris helped me with because I don't have any idea about what's about to happen to me." She began. "And I don't like to bother her that much because of what she's goin' through, you know what I mean?"

"But that's gonna be okay, tell her that I said so."

"I told her that too but you know how your mind wants to keep you in the negative all the time?"

"If you let it." "Aunt Frances gave me a scripture one day when I was talkin' to her and every time somethin' wants to bring me down, I think about this scripture she gave me."

"Probably somethin' deep huh?"

"Not really that deep but it makes sense." He said as he proceeded to pull Psalms 61 up on his phone for her to read.

"Hear my cry, o God, attend unto my prayer. She began to read quietly. "From the end of the earth will I cry unto thee, when my heart is overwhelmed: lead me to the rock that is higher than I."

"And when she first told me about that, I really didn't understand it until I started givin' stuff up that I couldn't handle." He said. "I'm learnin' how to let go of people that're tryin' to bring me down and it works."

"I'm not doin' anything like that am I?" Janice cautiously asked him.

"Sweetheart if that was the case, I would've found a way to let you know by now, put that out of your mind."

"I'm just makin' sure because I know that my mother is gonna be askin' me all kinds of questions about what's goin' on with us."

"Would it help if I talk to her as soon as she gets settled and has the time to really talk like I did with Marie?"

"It might, I'll let you know if that would make any difference to her." She said as she noticed Marie and Kathryn get off the elevator then.

"I didn't know that she was in a wheelchair." Michael said as he helped her stand before they walked towards them.

"I think she can walk without it but if she gets really tired, she'll use it." Janice said as Marie waved after spotting them.

"Oh my God, my baby's havin' a baby." Kathryn remarked a minute later after they embraced. "I wouldn't miss this for the world." She added as she noticed the change in Janice's appearance. "When is your due date again?"

"I still have another two months to go but I'm usin' that time to get stuff ready."

"Not without me you aren't, that's why I decided to do this so don't try to do everything by yourself." She told her. "And you're Michael?" She asked him, interrupting he and Marie.

"Yes ma'am." He said as he felt her analytical stare "size him up".

"You look just like your brother and I guess you're used to hearin' that aren't you?" She asked him as she slowly got up from the wheelchair. "We'll talk later." She told him without giving him the chance to answer her question.

"Do you need any help?" He asked her.

"I've got it, I'm used to this now." She told him with an air of resentment. "What you can do though is help us with all of these bags that I had to bring so make yourself useful."

"I called Donna and told her that we're here Michael, thanks for comin' out here to get us." Marie told him as she felt the need to diffuse their conversation after overhearing the exchange between them. "She said she ordered two pizzas so I'm glad we didn't eat on the plane."

"Randy can take all of her bags upstairs when he gets here Michael, just leave 'em right there." Donna told him an hour later after he brought Marie and Kathryn's luggage in from James and Chris' van.

"Are you sure, it's not a problem."

"Yeah Michael I'm sure, come on in here and get a couple of pieces of pizza, you deserve it." She said as she took his arm and started leading him into the kitchen.

"Am I in trouble?" He asked her a minute later as he sat down with the boys at the table.

"How are you gonna be in trouble, don't be paranoid." She said as she opened a two liter bottle of pop. "I just don't wanna see you in the middle of some mess between Janice and Kathryn." She began.

"Marie sent me a text and asked me to talk to you because I know you a little better than she does and I guess she could tell that she's already started in on you."

"And you know what?"

"What?" She asked him as she sat down across from him. "Stop it Brian, hurry up and finish that and stop playin' with it."

"I've already braced myself for a bumpy ride with this and my guard is up, you know what I mean?"

"What are you expectin'?"

"I already know what went down in there a few months ago with her and Douglas so why should I be any different?" Michael said. "I hope it doesn't go that far but you never know." He said, laughing a little.

"Did he tell you about that?"

"James told me about it one night when we were talkin' about some stuff." "And I know better than to bring it up with Douglas because once somethin' is done, it's done and he doesn't like to drag things back up."

"Bless his heart, I'll be glad when I get to that place because things like that will take me places that I don't wanna go." She admitted. "The Lord is helpin' me, pray for me."

"Everybody is dealin' with somethin', don't feel bad about that." Michael said as he opened one of the pizza boxes. "But I will say this much." He said pausing.

"What Michael?"

"I think that we've gotten to the point of no return and it's not gonna matter what she says or does to try to undo this." He said with quiet confidence.

"I think you're serious." Donna told him.

"As a heart attack as your mama says." He said, referring to Frances.

"And it might sound strange to you but the closer she gets to havin' this baby, the more determined I am to prove to her how serious I am about this."

"I wouldn't call it strange but it is pretty unusual because there's so many guys out there that don't want anything to do with their own kids."

"Sometimes I don't understand it myself but it is what it is." He said. "And the way that I've been prayin' about this, I can't go wrong."

"They sent me a e-mail yesterday that said your unit is supposed to be ready Sunday but I can borrow somebody's car and we can go take a look at the model if you want to." Marie told Kathryn upstairs in the guest room.

"How come you're just now sayin' somethin', we could've had what's his name stop on the way here." She said irritably as she slowly sat down on one of the beds.

"Because I don't check my e-mails everyday and his name is Michael mother, is it that hard for you to say?" Marie asked her while watching for Janice's reaction.

"I'm not gonna let myself get close to him because too much can happen with that, you know what I mean?"

"That doesn't have anything to do with now and if this is the way it's gonna be, maybe this wasn't such a good idea." Marie told her with as much grace and patience as she allowed her spirit to give her. "You don't have any reason to be comin' down on him because he hasn't done anything but be there for her and I think you know that mother."

"I know what it looks like and anybody can talk Marie." "I've been around a little longer than you have and I don't want her to be hurt any more than she has to be."

"Then if that happens, I'll deal with it." Janice spoke up then. "Are we goin' to see your place?" She asked her, purposely changing the subject.

"We'll wait until tomorrow, I'm too tired for all of that tonight." Kathryn said as she suddenly began to go back to the night of her accident. "You know if you had stayed home in the first place, none of us would be goin' through all of this, do you know how much pain I'm in right now because you decided that you weren't comin' back home like you should have?"

"I thought we talked about this before we left mother, there's no point in you always goin' back to that." Marie told her. "It happened and you really need to be thankful that you made it out of it as well as you did." She added as she noticed Janice get up and leave the room.

"So is she goin' back downstairs to be with him instead of stayin' up here with me?" "I thought she wanted me here with her while she's gettin' ready for the baby." She said, close to tears.

"She does, she's really tryin' to make up for the way she acted with you before, but you're runnin' her off." "And if you're not careful, she's not gonna want anything to do with you because you keep blamin' all of this on her and that's really unfair."

"Why is it unfair, if she had just come back home with me where she belonged, all of this mess that I'm in now wouldn't have happened." She insisted.

"Okay mother listen to me." Marie said as she sat down on the bed next to her. "Let's just think about this for a second."

She didn't answer but sat there shaking her head.

"Think back to how you reacted when she told you that she was pregnant."

"We were upset, do you know how that would have looked to everybody?"

"We're not talkin' about everybody else right now, you need to think about how you almost forced her here in the first place." Marie calmly told her. "You ran her away because you were selfish and self righteous about the whole thing and that's how she ended up here."

"And then when she got here, everybody probably turned her against me just because I wanted her to come back home."

"Nobody turned her against you but she found out what it felt like to be loved and there's no way that she was gonna go back to D.C. where she got used up and messed up by people that didn't care how she felt."

"Then why didn't you let her move in with you and Jerry?"

"Because nobody bothered to tell me what was goin' on 'til the accident happened." "She told me later on that she talked to you on Saturday, you blew up and told her to find someplace else to go."

Marie continued. "She had a little money saved up and that's how she bought a one way plane ticket and told 'Nita that she would be here that Sunday night and she's been here ever since so put yourself in her place for once mother."

"I'm really tryin' to understand but you're not the one that has to live with what I do day in and day out Marie."

"And I hate what happened to you but we can't go back and undo that day but feelin' sorry for yourself and blamin' Janice for it is not changin' a thing." Marie told her. "She got herself together with the help of a lot of people here and you really need to thank the Lord for Douglas because I think he's had more influence on her than anybody else has and for you to come here and try to pull her back down would be absolutely horrible and I'm not gonna let it happen." She said with authority.

"Why wasn't he the one to pick us up?"

"He offered to but Janice told him that Michael wanted to meet you right away so that's why." "And if it gets back to him that you might be tryin' to start some stuff with her, you're gonna be sorry that you went there."

"I'm her mother and he can't stop me from talkin' to her if I feel like things need to be said."

"And he's her father because both of us know that she didn't have one for the first eighteen years of her life." "He's stepped up and let God help him fill in that void so don't try to mess with that either." She concluded as she noticed her begin to shut out her words. "Did you remember to take your medicine before we left D.C.?"

"I think I did and it's makin' me drowsy so I'm gonna lay here for a few minutes." She said as she slowly began to lie down on the bed.

"You probably need to but just think about what I said and everybody will be better off."

"I know the Lord is helpin' me because a couple of months ago I would've been ready to go at it with her." Janice remarked at the table with Michael, Marie and Donna ten minutes later.

"You did the right thing but after you left, I had to give her a few things to think about so you might not hear about that stuff anymore." Marie said. "But I'm gonna leave that alone and keep prayin' for her, sometimes that's the only thing that works."

"How did that come up anyway?" Donna asked.

"She likes to blame other people for the things that she's goin' through right now but a lot things you bring on yourself." Marie said. "And I'm far from perfect and I've done the same thing when stuff goes wrong but God is teachin' me to take a look at myself before I start blamin' somebody else."

"I didn't know she was on medication." Janice remarked.

Marie nodded. "When she got done with rehab, they told me that she asked for somethin' that would help her because she felt depressed all of the time so her doctor put her on Prozac."

"But when you look at all of the stuff that's happened to her this year, it's easy to see why she would feel like that but that's the difference in knowin' where your help is comin' from." Donna said.

"I don't have nothin' against that because I've been there but when I say somethin' to her about seekin' the Holy Ghost, she'll shut me down real quick."

"And when it's like that, back off and let the Lord deal with her." Donna said. "I learned that when I tried to talk to Randy's mother one time."

"I found that out too because that just antagonizes her big time so 'til she brings it up, I'm not sayin' a word about that." Marie said. "I remember when it was me that was the same way so she's just keepin' me on my knees." She concluded.

"That's the way to go so whatever goes down, the Lord has my back and I'm up to whatever is comin' down my street." Michael said. "Bring it on."…

July 17, Friday

"I got a call from the doctor's office today where your mother had her tests done and I've been called on the carpet as they say."

Douglas remarked Friday evening as he sat down at the kitchen table with Paul and Jane.

"That's different, what's goin' on with that?" Jane asked him, obviously curious.

"It is different but when you find out how this happened, it makes more sense."

"Florence called me one day at work last week and wanted to know what your last name is." He told him. "And I spaced it, I forgot to tell you about it." Paul told Jane then.

"Okay back up, maybe I'm slow but go back to the beginnin.'" Jane said.

"She called me one day last week and wanted to know what Douglas' last name is and she didn't tell me why and I didn't ask her, I was too busy for those kinds of details." Paul said as they laughed at him.

"Evidently, her doctor's office called her wantin' to know because they're plannin' on publishin' her case in the A.M.A. journal." Douglas said then.

"And they need to get your input or somethin'?"

"That's pretty much it but I told them that I'd talk to 'em on one condition." He began as she sat a cup of coffee in front of him.

"Let me guess, they can't use your name?"

"That might not be a problem as long as they publish what I have to say and they're gonna get an earful."

"When her X-rays came back that day, they said that they were gonna do this but I didn't really expect to hear from 'em again." Jane said. "Did they tell you what they wanna know from you?"

"They weren't specific about that but I have a good idea about what they wanna know and it's not a mystery, she was healed by God through the power of prayer, end of story."

"But Douglas you and me know that because we were there, but this was stage three cancerous tumors on her lung and that's not somethin' that they see everyday."

"I know it's not but how do you put limitations on what God will do when your faith is in the right place?" He asked her. "And if they ask me what happened, I don't have a choice but to give God the glory for it."

"They can't deny that because they have the proof right there in front of 'em. Jane said. "And sometimes she'll come out and ask me if that really happened to her and she wonders why it was her and not some of her friends that have died from some of the same stuff."

"You should tell her that she was in the right place at the right time." Paul remarked. "The Lord knows how to get your attention and I would be tryin' to find out what was up with that."

"She really is tryin' to figure it all out but if I try to throw too much at her at one time, she'll back off and that's the last thing I want." Jane said then. "And I started to call you one day to see if you had a few minutes to talk to her because I'm too close to it, you know what I mean?"

"I do, and the next time she's out here and you get the feelin' that she needs to talk, call me."

"I just might do that and one day she almost had me laughin' in her face but she was serious." Jane said, starting to laugh at the thought. "She said what is that gentlemen's name again that prayed for me?" "Then she said if he didn't look so intimidating I would like to talk to him some more." She added. "Douglas intimidating?" "You've got to be kiddin.'"

"How long ago was this?" He asked as they laughed together.

"Maybe a week ago and I know that you're a busy man so I told her that the best place and time would be at church.

"When does she usually come over here?"

"She'll usually call on Saturday mornin' to let me know she's on her way but if that's a bad time, I'll let her know."

"There's no such thing as a bad time when it comes to souls so just let me know if she brings it up again." He said as Patti quietly knocked on the screened door.

"C'mon in honey, are you ok?" Jane asked her after noticing the look of fear on her face.

"Another angel said somethin' to me." She said as she looked over at Douglas as she remembered the incident a few months before. "And

I told 'Nita and she told me to come over here because you would believe me."

"She must've seen your van in the driveway." Paul remarked. "James took Chris and mother out to dinner so they're not there."

"Go talk to her Douglas, I don't think she wants an audience." Jane told him then.

"C'mere sweetheart." Douglas told her as he got up from the table and led her back out the door.

"Can you tell me exactly what you saw and heard?" Douglas asked her a minute later as they sat down at the picnic table between the two houses.

"'Nita told me to go in the chicken house to see if there was any more eggs out there." She began.

"Did this happen today?" Douglas asked her as he gradually gained her trust.

"It was after daddy and mom left and 'Nita didn't believe me when I told her what I saw." She said in frustration.

"I don't want you to worry about that part of it because it doesn't matter who doesn't believe you as long as you know it happened." He told her after a moment as he gave her his undivided attention.

"When I opened that door over there it was a lady that told me to tell my mom that her baby got healed." She said with straightforward childlike sincerity as she looked at him with pleading eyes, hoping to be believed.

"Was there anything else you heard?" He asked her as he attempted to keep his composure after hearing her words.

"The lady didn't say nothin' after that and I went back in the house and I told 'Nita what happened and she didn't believe me." She repeated.

"Did your mom tell you that somethin' was wrong?" Douglas asked her as he continued to patiently question her in order to get a complete understanding of her experience.

"She told me that we were gonna have another sister or brother."

"Did she tell you that it's two?" He asked her as he took the liberty of telling her about the twins.

"It's twins?" "Like Jay and Suzanne?" She asked, obviously surprised. "We're gonna have two twins?" She asked him as she held up two fingers. "How come they're sick?"

"Honey they're not sick, don't you remember what you just told me?"

"That they got healed?"

"Isn't that what your angel just told you?" He asked her in an effort to help her grasp the concept of faith.

She nodded.

"Then that's exactly what happened so don't let anybody else tell you anything different." He told her. "Do you remember some of the stories that you've learned about in Sunday school about how Jesus healed people that were sick and had other things wrong with them?" He asked as he noticed her countenance brighten as she began to relate to his words.

"Like the man that was blind and Jesus put dirt in his eyes and made him see?" She asked him after thinking a moment.

"You're exactly right and when He knows that you believe what He says, that's when He does things like that." He assured her. "Is there anything else that you need to talk about?"

"When can I tell mom what that lady told me?"

"Do you want to do that tonight when she gets back?"

"Can I?"

"Don't you think it'll make her happy to hear that?" He asked her, intrigued by the way she was being used by the Lord to be such a blessing in the situation.

She nodded then as he decided to end their conversation to prevent her from being overwhelmed with more information than she could process.

"Don't you think she might be watchin' too many "Touched By an Angel" reruns Douglas?" 'Nita asked him ten minutes later after he walked Patti back to the house.

"Is that what you think it is?" He asked her as she stood at the counter making a pitcher of lemonade.

"I don't know but sometimes I think they say and do things for attention." "And don't get me wrong, just because I don't have the Holy Ghost yet doesn't mean that I don't believe in all of that stuff but this is the second time she's said that she saw an angel." She said with skepticism. "Did she tell you what I said?" She asked him, laughing.

"She told me that you didn't believe her."

"I sort of do and sort of don't, does that make any sense?"

"You might not believe it but it doesn't do any good to tell her that." Douglas said as he noticed a text coming through on his phone.

"If that's James, I told him to text you, I said that you had somethin' to tell him and Chris." She said with a hint of sarcasm.

"I want her to tell them the same thing she told me so it's not up to me and he said they're on their way back." He said after reading the message. "I'm goin' back over to Paul and Jane's, I told him to call me when they get here."

"What's goin' on Douglas and please don't give me any bad news." Chris remarked half an hour later as he came up on the deck where she and Frances were sitting at the table.

"Do I look like I have bad news?" He asked her as Frances motioned for him to sit next to her. "Where's James?"

"He's in there with the kids, this is my day off."

"Can you have him and Patti come out here?"

"If you say so but you're scarin' me now, no kiddin.'" She said as she got up.

"What's goin' on honey, you can tell me." Frances told him then.

"I'm gonna tell you because it's you then I want you to listen to this child and tell me what you think." Douglas answered her. "She said to me that an angel wanted her to tell her mother that her baby was healed and my question to you is this." He continued as she immediately lifted her hands up in praise to God at what she had just heard from him.

"Keep talkin' honey, it's got to be good from here on out." She said as she held on to his arm.

"Have either Chris or James told any of the kids about what they found when she had her sonogram a couple of weeks ago?"

"I told 'em not to because they're too young to understand what's goin' on but I think Chris told 'Nita and Janice then she dared 'Nita to say anything." "We all know how she is and I think she got the message but this child could tell that somethin' was startin' to look different about Chris and she just came out and told her but that's as far as it went."

"Then that pretty much tells me that she's not makin' this up." "I know that kids have imaginations about things and 'Nita said somethin' about her watchin' too many "Touched By an Angel" reruns, but we could tell when she showed up at Paul and Jane's over there that somethin' was goin' on."

"So all of this went on when were gone tonight?" Frances asked as she continued to hold on to him.

"Yes ma'am, and I'm sayin' too much, I want you to hear her for yourself and then tell me what you think." He said as Chris, James and Patti came out of the house then.

"Do I get to tell 'em now?" She asked as she went straight to Douglas for instruction.

"Go ahead, tell them the same things that you told me." He urged her.

"Did you do somethin' that you weren't supposed to and you're afraid to tell us?" Chris asked her.

"'Nita told me to go out to the chicken house to see if there was some eggs and it was a angel in there that told me to tell you that the baby got healed." She said as she started to tremble again at the thought of what she had experienced.

At that, both Chris and James looked at Douglas for his reaction at what she had just spoken to them.

"Honey you don't have anything to be afraid of, calm yourself down." Frances said as she put her arm around her as she stood between she and Douglas. "Go over there and give your mama and daddy a hug because I think they need one and tell them it's all okay now." She added as Douglas sat there speehless as he watched their reaction to her words while they began to feel the presence of God among them.

"When did this happen Patti?" James managed to ask her as Chris broke down in his arms as her spirit began to bear witness at the word that had been sent to them from the mouth of their child.

"When you and mommy and went out for dinner." She said after a moment as she attempted to think about the timeline.

"So this just happened tonight?" He asked her.

"Yes sir." She said.

"Can you show us where exactly this happened sweetheart?" Douglas asked her as Frances went over to take Chris back in the house.

She nodded. "It was in the chicken house over there." She said as she pointed to it, twenty five yards away from where they were.

"I sat down with her right after she showed up at Paul and Jane's back door and she told me basically what she said a few minutes ago." Douglas remarked as he and James followed behind Patti as she walked towards the chicken house. "And if she was makin' this up, where did she get the healing part from?" "Mother said your kids don't have any idea what was goin' on, you know what I mean?"

"I'm still tryin' to process this, let me think about that for a second." James said, shaking his head at what they had just heard.

"Just don't make it harder than it has to be James." He told him. "When we prayed and asked the Lord to do this work didn't you ask in faith?"

"Yeah we did." He said as he recalled the night that he had ministered to he and Chris.

"Then this shouldn't be a surprise to any of us but I do understand that we weren't expectin' anything like this." He added as they slowed down while approaching the small five hundred square foot structure.

"I saw her right there." Patti told them a minute later as she pointed to the east side corner.

"Do you remember what she looked like?" Douglas asked her.

"She had on a black dress and she told me not to be afraid of her." She immediately recalled. "Then she told me to tell my mother that her baby was healed." She repeated to him.

"Okay baby, that's all we need to know." James told her. "Did you forget to take all of these eggs?" He asked, noticing several scattered on the straw floor.

"When she told me that I went to tell 'Nita what she said and I forgot." She said as she got the "egg box" from the nearby shelf.

"Meet me at the house, I'm gonna go talk to Chris for a minute." Douglas said as he left them. "Keep talkin' to her."

"Haven't you ever prayed about somethin' and then be shocked when you get your answer?" Chris asked Douglas as they sat in the family room with Frances ten minutes later.

"I think all of us have had that happen but when you think about it, couldn't you say that's unbelief when it comes down to it?" He asked her. "And I'll be the first one to say it, I've been guilty so that's when I started to get really hard on myself because I refuse to have my prayers hindered because I'm doubtin' God about somethin.'"

"And that comes from leanin' on your own understanding." Frances said then. "Our natural minds will tell us every time that this or that can't or won't happen because of the way things might look but because of the Holy Ghost, we're supposed to have the mind of Christ so what's the problem?"

"It shouldn't be a problem and what we've seen the Lord do in the last month should be enough to really let us know that there's nothin' too hard for Him to do." Douglas said. "When do you go back to the doctor?"

"Monday afternoon." Chris said still absorbing what she had heard. "And I don't like it because my mind is still tryin' to tell me that none of that happened with her because it's just too bizarre." She said. "And I'm just keepin' it real."

"Then you need to let God help your mind because what you're about to see is real." Frances told her with authority. "What were you thinkin' when you asked the Lord to do this?"

"I probably had in my mind that we were gonna go in there and they would see that everything's okay with 'em so this is totally different." She said as she wiped tears from her face. "Are we keepin' you from doin' somethin' else Douglas?"

"Not hardly, Irene is with Marie and Janice tryin' to get Kathryn ready to move to her new place Sunday so she told me to take my time." "We split up the kids so don't worry about it, she would want me here with you and James so it's all good ma'am." He said.

"And you need to stop tryin' to handle everything by yourself because that's not how the Lord meant for it to be." Frances told her. "And this is a wonderful thing that God has done so actually, you need to be rejoicin' about it instead of worryin' about how He's doin' it."

"We're not really used to seein' things like this but God doesn't change, and if He saw fit to use your child again to send you a message, then so be it." Douglas told her. "And evidently, she has somethin' extra that the Lord sees in her that's gonna go a long way."

"Are you prophesyin' about my daughter?" Chris asked him, laughing a little.

"I'm not goin' that far but when I was with her before you got back, I noticed that she seems to have a really good understandin' about what she's been taught so far and that goes a long way." Douglas told her. "So whatever you're doin', pay just a little more attention to that one because there's probably more comin' from her and you heard it here first."...

JULY 19, SUNDAY

"Since I have to leave tomorrow, we decided to cook here instead of goin' out to the country for dinner." Marie remarked after Janice and Kathryn came in from walking around the grounds of Edencrest Village Sunday afternoon.

"So this was what you didn't wanna tell me huh?" Kathryn asked Janice as she she slowly sat down.

"We didn't want you to have to eat in the cafeteria your first night here so we went to the store while you were at Donna's house Friday night." Marie said as she finished making up a salad. "And I asked

Michael to come too, he'll be here when he gets done with his church bus route."

"So whose idea was that?" Kathryn asked her.

"I think it would be a good thing if you sit down and talk to him and get everything out in the open so it was my idea." Marie said without holding back. "And nobody is askin' you to act like he's your favorite person in the world but he's probably gonna be your son-in-law so it might be a good idea to get to know him."

"What do you need me to do until he gets here?" Janice asked her as she opened the refrigerator. "He just texted me and told me he's on his way."

"if you can make the gravy for the potatoes, that'll be the last thing that needs to be done." Marie said as she washed her hands at the sink. "So did you get a chance to see most of the grounds around here?" She asked her as she came over to sit down next to her on the sofa.

"We saw about half of it because I couldn't move that fast, my hip can't take too much but what I saw is beautiful." She admitted.

"Are you gonna call me a couple of times a week to let me know how you're doin'?"

"If I think about it, I'm gonna be busy makin' sure Janice is ready for this baby because it's not that far off." "That's why I made this move."

"I know it is but she's pretty much on top of it, you haven't seen her nursery yet have you?"

"Who helped you out with that, Christine?" She asked Janice with an air of resentment.

"She helped me make a list of what I needed to buy because I have no clue about that kind of stuff." Janice said in her defense.

"So after the baby is born, you won't need me around because you're still livin' with her and James." She threw at her. "Don't you think it's gonna really be crowded there with all of their kids and yours too?"

"Do you have any idea how big their house is?" Marie asked her. "James made sure that they have enough room when they were buildin' that house so that's not an issue mother." She added. "Please stop tryin' to start stuff." She said as she resisted the urge to "put her in her place."

"Maybe you and Michael should start thinkin' about movin' in together since you think you might be marryin' him so he'll be able to see what's really goin' on."

"We're not doin' that." Janice said.

"I don't know why not." She insisted. "If you don't, both of you are gonna be sorry and I'll say somethin' to him about it if you don't."

"He'll tell you the same thing so if I were you, I wouldn't go there." Marie told her. "There he is and I'm just askin' you not to start anything with him, this is not the time and place." She said after he knocked on the door. "Just try to chill out."

"Janice didn't tell me that you're from St. Louis, what made you move up here?" Kathryn asked Michael ten minutes later after the four of them had sat down at the table.

"The job that I had down there closed up the plant and I called Douglas out of desperation one day to see if I might have a chance of findin' somethin' up here."

"So where is it that you're workin' now, what were you able to find?" She asked, hoping that he would feel the pressure behind her questions.

"I'm one of the dock supervisors at a furniture warehouse on the east side; the best job I've ever had and I know exactly where it came from."

"Did you have somebody that you know sneak you in ahead of everybody else?" "That's usually how it works, it's not what you know but who you know that gets you places."

"I'll put it like this." He began as he poured more iced tea in his glass. "When I moved up here I didn't know anybody except Douglas and he didn't have anything to do with how it all came together."

"Wasn't it one of those things where God showed up and showed out?" Marie asked him.

"And you know it, Aunt Frances still doesn't know how much she had to do with that job comin' through but I know better." He said thinking back. "Somehow me and my pity party ended up at her house one day and she got busy." "Between her and the Lord, I had a job in less than three days so nobody can tell me that prayer doesn't work."

"You would've probably gotten the job anyway, I don't think Frances had anything to do with it." Kathryn said then with an angry edge in her voice.

"But anyway, that's where I am and that's what I do." He said before pausing as he gathered his thoughts while refusing to argue with her last comment. "And I know that you have the right to know what I'm about because I'm in Janice's life."

"You can be in her life all that you want but my main question to you is what makes you think you're gonna be willin' to take care of a baby that doesn't belong to you?" "This may be my only grandchild and I'm not gonna sit back and let a perfect stranger kick her to the curb one day because she doesn't belong to you."

"And you know what?" "I have enough sense to know that it doesn't matter what I say about it because talk is cheap so I'm not goin' there." Michael answered her as their eyes met. "This is between us so there's not really much else that can be said, you know what I mean?"

"No, this is between the three of us because this is my daughter and I'm not about to lose her again." "I almost lost my life a few months ago tryin' to make things right and I'm not about to go through that again." She said as Janice got up from the table.

"I'm startin' to think this was a mistake because if this is what she's gonna be doin', we're gonna have some problems." Janice remarked five minutes later as she and Marie walked around the grounds.

"I asked her not to do exactly what she's doin' and I could tell that Michael is doin' everything he can to take it so don't worry about him, he's got it under control."

"He told me that he's been prayin' about this because he knew it was comin.'" Janice said. "And I got up and came out here because I could tell where she was goin.'"

"He can take care of himself because he's probably gotten a heads up from Douglas so don't worry about it." Marie told her. "Don't argue with her about anything because that's what causes a lot of confusion and hurt feelings and all of that and that's the last thing you need."

"Tell me about it so if she wants to get me to talk about what's goin' on with us, I'll just tell her that I don't know yet and I really don't." "Too much can happen."

"You still have your guard up don't you?"

"It's better than it used to be and I love how he's not puttin' any kind of pressure on me to do anything but I know somethin' is gonna have to happen pretty soon one way or another." "I'm not that stupid to take him for granted like that."

"Do you know how much all of this has matured you in the last six months?" Marie asked her as they stopped and sat down on a bench.

"Somebody else told me that but I don't have much choice, I can't act like I'm fifteen with a baby to take care of."

"Are you scared of what you're about to go through?"

"I used to be but Chris has explained to me so much of what's gonna be happenin' and it's really not that deep when you think about it."

"So what exactly happened with Patti Friday night?" Marie asked her.

"Who told you about it, Irene?"

"When Douglas came to pick her and the kids up from Donna's house, I kind of overheard some stuff but it was late and I didn't get it all."

"She told Douglas and James that 'Nita sent her to the hen house to see if there were any eggs to bring in." She said after thinking a moment. "Then she saw what she says was an angel that told her to tell her mother that her babies were healed."

"Just like the night I almost messed myself up." Marie said. "She said an angel told her to come downstairs and if she hadn't, I might not be here."

166

"That is so awesome and that's the kind of thing you just hear about but when stuff like happens arounds us, it's even better."

"So when does Chris go back to the doctor?"

"Tomorrow and she told me when she gets back home, we're gonna have a party to celebrate." Janice said. "She's really been goin' through with what they told them and I've never seen her so out of it and it was a little strange."

"Irene told me that she's been on the internet tryin' to find out what was goin' on and that can't help anything." Marie commented. "And one night I think James told her to just stop it because it was puttin' pictures in her mind that didn't need to be there."

"Aunt frances told her not to let the devil have a field day in her mind and that she wasn't let her faith work like it's supposed to." Janice said, amused. "But I've been puttin' myself in her place and she's the only one that's actually goin' through it and it's so easy for everybody else to tell you not to feel a certain way."

"Because she's the only one carryin' those babies and I've never been pregnant but that can't be easy."

"It's not and I know what it feels like now to worry about stuff goin' wrong with your baby." Janice said, shaking her head a little. "And I told Michael that if somethin' would happen with her or if she was born sick, I don't want him to feel like he has to stick around."

"And I think I already know what he said too." Marie said.

"Did he say anything to you about that?"

"He hasn't but I think I'm startin' to understand where he's comin' from and believe me, he's had time to change his mind about this."

"Then if you can see it, why is she havin' such a hard time with him?" Janice asked, referring to Kathryn.

"I think that she's tryin' to give him a chance but she's had so many bad relationships in her life and she doesn't want to see you go through the things that she did." Marie said after a moment. "And I'm not defendin' the way she's puttin' him through the third degree but she's tryin' to find out how real he is."

"But a lot of things have to happen before she can see that and I just wish she would back off of him for a minute."

"Do you think it would help if somebody else besides us would talk to her?"

"Like who?" "She already has her mind made up and I don't think she'll listen to anybody else."

"If the right person gets to her, she might so don't give up on her honey and both of know now what the Lord can do so give her to God and go on."

"Aunt Frances told me one time that's what she did with Douglas, he was too much for her so she gave him to the Lord."

"We know how that turned out so don't get discouraged about her and when it comes down to it, this is between you and Michael." "It doesn't really matter what other people think about what he's doin'."

"I know, Chris told me that same thing." "And this might sound crazy but sometimes I feel sort of guilty because I don't think I deserve him."

"Why not?"

"Because of the way I acted before the Lord started straightenin' me out."

"Before the Holy Ghost huh?"

"And you know it, this time last year I was out of control so it just feels like things shouldn't be workin' out like they are."

"It's called grace and none of us deserve it so just thank God and keep goin' like you are." "Take it one day at a time.".....

"They called me Friday and said that both of our background checks came back clean and clear." Sheila remarked at the table with Douglas, Terry and Frances.

"And that is crazy, I just knew that stuff from St. Louis was gonna show up." Terry said.

"So what does that tell you?" Douglas asked her then.

"That I'm supposed to be doin' somethin' at Second chance because if I wasn't, all kinds of mess would've shown up." She answered after thinking a moment.

"When they called me, they asked me when we wanted to come and we decided a week from today would be the best time because both of us are off from work."

"Whatever you do, make sure you pray before you go because you don't know what you're walkin' into." Douglas told them. "You're doin' the right thing by respondin' to a need but you don't wanna get into somethin' that you can't handle either."

"Have you ever done that?"

"I can remember the first time I tried to explain what the Holy Ghost is to one of my crack house friends that came by to see what happened to me." He began. "What I had was a lot of zeal and not much knowledge."

"Do you remember what you told him?" Sheila asked, fascinated.

"I told him that he wouldn't be seein' me again because I didn't need the stuff anymore and I wasn't gonna be messin' up other people with it either."

"He probably didn't believe you either did he?"

"You're right, he didn't." "He told me that I'd be back in a couple of months and he'd be waitin' on me."

"You think he has the message by now?"

"The last time I saw him was downtown at the city county building, he was on his way to court for somethin' that he had gotten involved in." He said after a moment. "That was probably two years ago and I talked to him for a few minutes before he had to go in the court room with his lawyer."

"So what was is reaction when he saw you again?"

"He was pretty much in shock and I don't say that because of anything I've done."

"C'mon Douglas, we know you better than that." Sheila told him as she put a slice of watermelon on her plate.

"I know you do but it doesn't hurt to say it every now and then." He remarked. "And when you go to talk to these souls, the last thing you wanna do is give them the impression that you're lookin' down on 'em or that you think you're better than they are." "You're there to let

169

them know what God will do when they take a first step and there's nothin' better than your own testimony to move people."

"And that's what made them call me back." Sheila said. "Nobody did any preachin' that night but it was Terry's testimony that they can't forget about." "Then on top of that, what happened between her and Andre' was out of this world and they just want more of that."

"And you have the power to give them what they're lookin' for because that's part of the reason why the Lord gave you His spirit.' Frances told her. "And you already know that because you've been around for a little bit but that's what this baby right here needs to hear." She said as she touched Terry's arm.

"I just wish I could explain to everybody around here how much help you've been to me." She said as her mind began to go back to her history. "And I just wannna be able to help somebody else because I know what it's like to need it and nobody else cares."

"But the Lord knew and that's why you eneded up where you did." Frances told her. "So what you need to do is keep tellin' people how He's able to meet you where you are and what they're hungry for is what you already have so don't hold back on what God has done for you."

"There is no way because I almost died and I don't want anybody else to go through that." She said.

"Sweetheart God knows that and He will give you the right words to say and the let you know what to do so don't be afraid of it." Frances continued. "And like your big brother just told the both of you, make sure you pray before you go and that way, you don't have any choice but to be used by God." She said as Jane and Florence walked in.

"This is dessert if anybody wants it." Jane said as she sat a pan of cherry cobbler on the counter.

"If that's not right on time I don't know what is." Sheila said as she noticed Florence hesitating to sit down at the table with them. "Are you gonna have some with us?" She asked her as she noticed the only empty chair next to Douglas. "He doesn't bite."

"I'm harmless, you know that by now." He told her as he held the chair out for her. "Did Jane tell you about the phone call that I got the other day?" He asked.

"She did and I'm really curious about that." She said as she gradually allowed herself to be at ease with him.

"They'll probably ask me what happened with you and I don't have any choice but to let them know exactly what went on." He said after a moment.

"Do you think they'll believe you?"

"It doesn't really matter if they do or not, facts are facts." "You were healed by the power of God and there's not too much else I can say about it."

"Wait a minute, what did I miss?" Sheila asked. "Who is they?"

"My doctor's office called me last week and they would like some information from him about how things happened with me." She began. "They want to publish an article in the A.M.A. journal about it because it's so unbelievable."

"It's unbelievable when you leave God out of situations but as soon as you put some confidence in what His word says about faith, it's not as unbelievable as it seems." Douglas remarked then. "There are too many examples of what will happen when you ask and believe God because He can't lie or fail."

"It was impossible thing for the Red Sea to part too but with God, nothin' is impossible." She said with emphasis. "And we really shouldn't be surprised when He does things because He said there is nothin' too hard for him to do." Frances put in. "And Douglas, I'm sure when you go in there and talk to these people, you're not gonna mince words are you?"

"You know me too well ma'am but I know people too, especially the professionals and for the most part, they're skeptics." He answered. "But all I can do is tell them exactly what went on and when it comes down to it, they can take it or leave it."

"But how can they not believe it, you've got the proof right there with the X-rays." Sheila said. "One day they see lung cancer and the next time they look at it, there's no trace of it."

"Without chemo or radiation so what else could it be except the power of God?" Frances said. "It's pretty simple when you think about it but it's the ones that want to doubt that tear down faith and we can't let that happen." "Too much is goin' on for us not to be takin' authority over things because right before Jesus left here, He said that we would receive power after the Holy Ghost comes and that's not for us to sit down on it and act like it's not there."

"Is that why you told James to lay hands on Chris and heal his children?" Sheila asked Douglas. "When she told me that, I cried, I couldn't help it."

"You got it, God does the healing through our hands and I think so many times that we suffer with things that we don't have to."

"What's wrong with Christine?" Florence asked then.

"When she went to the doctor for her first sonogram a couple of weeks ago, they found out that she was carryin' conjoined twins." Frances told her.

"Oh my God." Florence said as she covered her mouth in shock. "What are they going to do?"

"When we found out what was goin' on, it was time to call on the name of the Lord, just like we did with your problem." Frances continued. "And we have our answer before she goes back for another examination so they're in for another surprise." She said with authority and confidence.

"But is that possible?" "Babies born that way have to be separated by surgery after they're born so how is that possible?" She asked again.

"It's possible because is there anything too hard for the Lord?" Douglas spoke up as he quoted the scripture from Genesis 18:14. "You can't limit God because of what things look like and He proved Himself to you so this is no different." He told her.

"I didn't mean to sound like I don't believe you but I've never heard of such a thing." She said then with an apologetic tone in her voice.

"Do you have a few minutes for me?" He asked her as he stood up and motioned for her to follow him out.

"I love it, he's about to help her out." Sheila said, laughing at what just happened. "That's why I love your brother, he doesn't let anything stop him from doin' what he has to do." She told Terry.

"Jane told me that you wanted to talk to me again, what can I do for you?" Douglas asked her a few minutes later as they sat down in the family room after he closed the French doors behind them.

"I really don't know where to start because I'm just a little overwhelmed with everything that has happened to me the last few weeks." She managed to say a few moments later as she nervously gathered her thoughts.

"I can understand that but I'm gonna ask you to calm yourself down because I'm not here to intimidate you or to make you feel uncomfortable." He told her. "And if that happens, let me know."

She nodded as she forced herself to make eye contact with him.

"What exactly is it that has you so overwhelmed?" He patiently asked her.

"I've been trying to understand why God did such a wonderful thing for me after all of the wrong things that I've done in the past."

"And you know what?" He asked her. "Sometimes we waste a lot of time tryin' to figure out the grace of God because our minds can't handle it." "The best thing for you to do is get to the place where you're ready to make a fresh start with the Lord and you can start by askin' Him for His spirit."

"His spirit?" She asked in a child like manner.

"God's spirit is the Holy Ghost and He promised it to you when you ask for it." He told her as he reached for France's bible that was sitting on one of the end tables. "Do you believe what's written in this book?"

"It's the Word of God isn't it?"

"Absolutely and because it is, you can't go wrong by doin' what it tells you to do." He began. "You're in a good place because you do believe it because a lot of people don't and they miss out on the best thing you can have in this life." He added as he turned to the eleventh chapter of Luke.

"Jane told me about how you came to know the Lord and it really surprised me because you're so different now from what she described to me." She told him then, becoming increasingly fascinated with his demeanor.

"I don't know how much she told you but I had to go through some rough stuff before the Lord got my attention about salvation." He said then. "I might take the time on another day to get into that but this is not about me right now." "I have to talk to you the way the Lord is leadin' me and I have a question for you."

She nodded.

"What do you feel about the way your body was healed?"

"Sometimes I can't believe that it actually happened to me and I wonder if there's another reason why I'm still here."

"You're still here because the Lord has more for you and it's a wonderful thing that you got your help but this right here is dyin' everyday." He said as he held up one of his hands, illustrating flesh. "And I'm sure that you already know that but my point is to help you to understand that it's more important for you to have salvation than it is for your body to be healed."

"Jane told me the same thing but I understand it a little better because of how you're breaking it down to me." Florence said as she began to feel at ease with him.

"It's easy to see when you get your own mind out of the way and it comes down to takin' God at His word because it's impossible for Him to lie." He told her.

"What do you want to show me?" She asked as she continued to cooperate with him.

"Start with verse nine and finish with verse thirteen and tell me what you get out of it." He said as he handed the bible over to her.

"And I say unto you, Ask, and it shall be given you; seek, and ye shall find; knock, and it shall be opened unto you." She began. "For every one that asketh receiveth; and he that seeketh findeth; and to him that knocketh it shall be opened." She continued as the simplicity of the verses began to make an impact on her.

"Keep goin' hon." He said as he noticed her countenance gradually began to illuminate as the words of Jesus ministered to the eternal unseen soul.

"If a son shall ask bread of any of you that is a father, will he give him a stone? Or if he ask a fish, will he give for a fish give him a serpent?" She read slowly in an effort to understand what she was reading. "Or if he shall ask an egg, will he offer him a scorpion?"

"And if you don't remember anything else that you just read, don't ever forget this one." He instructed her.

Again she nodded before she began reading the thirteenth verse. "If ye then, being evil, know how to give good gifts unto your children: how much more shall your heavenly Father give the Holy Spirit to them that ask him?" She finished as they began to feel the presence of God around them.

"What does that mean to you?" He gently and quietly asked her.

"It says that God will give me the Holy Spirit when I ask Him to." She said after hesitating a moment.

"That's exactly what it means and I'm not sayin' that because it's somethin' that I've heard about from somebody else." Douglas said. "I was fresh off the streets and after I saw a friend of mine lose his life right in front of me, it let me know that it could've been me that went into eternity without salvation and there's nothin' worse."

"Did that make you wonder why it was your friend that died instead of you?"

"I wasn't thinkin' that way at first; all I could think about was the way he died and because of that, I almost killed myself." He said as he thought back to twenty years earlier. "But because somebody took the time to explain to me and backed up what they were tellin' me in the scripture about how to be delivered from what I was goin' through, I can tell you that this is truth and it can't fail." He concluded.

Did someone tell you about this?"

"Yes ma'am." "There were two people that didn't know anything about me but they knew how hungry I was." He said as he remembered the details of his experience. "They made sure that I knew what the Lord would do when I made up my mind to leave my old life style behind me and let Him start me all over again." He said. "And what He did for me, He'll do the same thing for anybody else that cares about where they're gonna spend eternity."

"Is this what Jane has been talking to me about?"

"I'm sure it is and I don't know exactly what she's told you but I don't think she would hold anything back that would help you to understand what this is all about."

"She told me about how Jame's sister told her about how she came to know the Lord back when they were college roommates." She said.

"Did she tell you about the night she received the Holy Ghost when she came home with her on Christmas break?"

"I think that I remember her trying to explain that to me back when it first happened to her but that's been such a long time ago."

"That was probably about twenty five years ago before I even knew her but it's somethin' that you can never forget." He said. "There's nothin' anymore powerful in this world than to have the spirit of God come into your body and that's the promise that He made right before the Holy Ghost came on the Day of Pentecost."

"Is all of that in there too?"

"It is and if you're really interested in reading it for yourself, it's all here for you." Douglas said as he turned to the book of Acts.

"It's amazing that I haven't heard of this before now." Florence commented as she continued to closely watch him.

"You're not by yourself hon, I didn't have any idea what the Lord was about to do for me when I went to church just because Irene's mother told me to come and let God help me."

"She's really a sweet lady, I'm glad to know her."

"She's been a real blessin' to all of us and she knows how to help you believe God because of everything she's been through." He said as he found the first chapter and the eighth verse. "Jesus was talkin' to his disciples right before he left here after He was crucified and resurrected." "Read that for me." He said as he showed her the highlighted verse.

"But ye shall receive power, after that the Holy Ghost is come upon you: and ye shall be witnesses unto me both in Jerusalem and in all Judae'a and in Samaria, and unto the uttermost part of the earth."

"He was talkin' to his disciples that verse but when you go a little farther with it in the second chapter when that promise first happens in the upper room where they were waitin' for it."

"I've heard of the upper room from some of my friends that have been to Jerusalem."

"And it's still there and when you read the first four verses of this second chapter, it describes how it happened."

"Do you want me to read again?" She asked him.

"This isn't about what I want, this is about your desire to know what God has for you." He told her. "This truth is what your soul loves and it knows the difference between what's artificial and what the real thing is." "There are all kinds of things that people get involved in tryin' to fill a void but there's nothin' else like this that satisfies the soul and that's all that matters in the end."

"And when the day of Pentecost was fully come, they were al with one accord in one place." She began. "And suddenly there came a sound from heaven as of a rushing mighty wind, and it filled all the house where they were sitting." "And there appeared unto them cloven tongues like as of fire, and it sat upon each of them." She continued as she read it slowly in order to understand and visualize what she was reading.

"Have you ever heard of that before?"

"Jane has talked to me about it before but I don't think I've ever actually seen it happen."

"When God gives you his spirit, it will speak out of your mouth in another language and that's the evidence that you've been born again." Douglas told her without hesitation or apology. "Some people seem to have a problem with that but this is God's work and it can't be changed." "When it happened to me I thought that I would bust out of my body because it's that powerful."

"Is that the power that Jesus talked about in the other verse that I just read ?"

"I think you're gettin' it." He told her as they continued to feel the presence of God around them. "It's that power that helps you live the life of holiness that the Lord wants from the people that want to make it out of here when He comes back, that's the bottom line." He said as he took a handkerchief from his shirt pocket. "And I have one more scripture for you that pretty much sums it all for you when you believe it." He added as he showed her thirty eighth verse in the same chapter.

"Then Peter said unto them, Repent, and be baptized every one of you in the name of Jesus Christ for the remission of sins, and ye shall receive the gift of the Holy Ghost." She read with deliberation in order to comprehend what she was reading and it was then that they heard a faint knock on one of the doors before Sheila and Jane walked in with Patti who was fluently and unmistakably speaking in that unknown language that they had just spoken about.

The unique anointing of the Holy Ghost filled the room, confirming a repentant and believing heart, even in such a young child.

"We heard all this noise in the basement and the kids were down there playin' church and I've heard 'em do that before but it was somethin' different about it this time." Sheila said in tears as she, Jane and Douglas watched her walk around the room speaking in an unknown tongue, allowing God to have His way with her.

"Is this what we were just talking about?" Florence asked him as she sat in bewildered awe at what was happening.

"This is exactly it, you're seein' it for yourself." He said in amazement at yet another miracle in the household. "My God I love it." He added as the anointing of God saturated the atmosphere. "Where are Chris and James, they can't miss this." He asked Jane.

"Sheila went to find 'em, they're somewhere in here." She said as she sat down next to Florence.

"What's making this happen to her?" She asked, still in confusion. "She's just a child, isn't she afraid of this?"

"Mom this isn't anything to be afraid of, do you remember when I told you about the night this happened to me?" Jane quietly asked her while watching Patti circle the room, caught up in the spirit of God as He gave fluent utterance through her.

"What's goin' on?" Chris asked then as she and James came in through the doors.

"At that, no one spoke as they allowed them to discover what was transpiring with their second born child,barely nine years old.

For the promise is unto you, and to your children, and to all that are afar off, even as many as the Lord our God shall call. Acts2:39(KJV).

End of Part 3

Printed in the United States
By Bookmasters